Su-34

Russia's 4th+ Generation Strike Fighter

HUGH HARKINS

Copyright © 2019 Hugh Harkins

All rights reserved.

ISBN: 1-903630-45-2
ISBN-13: 978-1-903630-45-7

Su-34

Russia's 4th+ Generation Strike Fighter

© Hugh Harkins 2019

Centurion Publishing
United Kingdom

ISBN 10: 1-903630-45-2
ISBN 13: 978-1-903630-45-7

This volume first published in 2019

The Author is identified as the copyright holder of this work under sections 77 and 78 of the Copyright Designs and Patents Act 1988

Cover design © Centurion Publishing and KDP
Page layout, concept and design © Centurion Publishing

All rights reserved. No part of this publication may be reproduced, stored in a retrieval system, transmitted in any form, or by any means, electronic, mechanical or photocopied, recorded or otherwise, without the written permission of the publisher

The publisher and author would like to thank all organisations and services for their assistance and contributions in the preparation of this volume: Central Aerodynamic Institute; Concern Radio Electronic Technologies; FSUE Gas Turbine Engineering MMPP Salut; GNPP Region; GosMKB Vympel; JSC NPP Aerosilia; JSC Experimental Design Bureau Electroautomatics; JSC KNIRTI (Kaluga Research Radio Engineering Institute); JSC NPP Polet; JSC Research Institute for Instrumentation, Tikhomirov; JSC Tactical Missiles Corporation; JSC TsNPO Leninets; JSC UMOZ PO; KBP Tula; Ministry of Defence of the Russian Federation; Novosibirsk Aviation Plant. V.P. Chkalova; PJSC Sukhoi; PJSC UEC Saturn; Rosoboronexport; Scientific Production Enterprise Zvezda; Ufa Motor Building Association; United Aircraft Corporation

Citation guide: (TsAGI) Central Aerodynamic Institute; (Kret) Concern Radio Electronic Technologies; (MMPP Salut) FSUE Gas Turbine Engineering MMPP Salut; (GNPP Region) GNPP Region; (GosMKB Vympel) GosMKB Vympel; (Electroautomatics); JSC Experimental Design Bureau Electroautomatics; (KNIRTI) JSC KNIRTI (Kaluga Research Radio Engineering Institute); (Tikhomirov) JSC Research Institute for Instrumentation, Tikhomirov; (TMC) JSC Tactical Missiles Corporation; (KBP Tula) KBP Tula; (MODRF) Ministry of Defence of the Russian Federation; (NAZ) Novosibirsk Aviation Plant. V.P. Chkalova; (Sukhoi) PJSC Sukhoi; (UEC Saturn) PJSC UEC Saturn; (Rosoboronexport) Rosoboronexport; (NPP Zvezda) Scientific Production Enterprise Zvezda; (UMPO) Ufa Motor Building Association; (UAC) United Aircraft Corporation

CONTENTS

	Introduction	vii
1	Sukhoi T-10-T10V – Su-34 Genesis	1
2	T-10V Development to Su-34 Serial Production	17
3	Su-34 Fullback	43
4	Armament Options	91
5	Su-34 – Russian Aerospace Group, Syria Operations	121
6	Glossary	139

INTRODUCTION

The Sukhoi Su-34 'Fullback' strike fighter was developed from the Sukhoi Su-27 'Flanker' air superiority fighter as a $4^{th}+$ generation stike aircraft for service with the VKS – Russian Federation Air Force – from the second decade of the twenty first century. The Su-34 was designed to replace the Russian Federations aging fleet of Sukhoi Su-24M/2 variable-geometry strike aircraft and possibly the Su-24MR in the tactical reconnaissance role. Conceived under the T-10V program in the twilight years of the Soviet Union – Union of Soviet Socialist Republics – the design weathered the financial crisis that gripped Russia following the break-up of that union on 25 December 1991. The T-10V matured into an advanced strike aircraft, deliveries to the Russian Federation Air Force commencing in second half of the first decade of the twenty first century.

This volume covers the program from conception to operational service with chapters describing the aircraft design, development, production, systems, weapons complexes and strike operations flown by the Russian Aerospace Group supporting the Syrian Arab Republic in the civil war that gripped that nation in the 2010's.

1

SUKHOI T-10-T-10V – SU-34 GENESIS

Entering service with the VKS (Russian Federation Air Force) in 2014, the Sukhoi Su-34 – NATO (North Atlantic Treaty Organisation) reporting name 'Fullback' – was developed as a 4th+ generation tactical strike fighter (termed fighter bomber by the MODRF (Ministry of Defence of the Russian Federation) aircraft to replace the Soviet Union and later Russian Federation fleets of variable-geometry (swing-wing) Sukhoi Su-24M tactical strike aircraft. The Su-34, in excess of 100 of which had been delivered by 2018, was to be capable of conducting the full-spectrum of strike operations against land – fixed and mobile – and sea surface targets in single aircraft or group operations in fair and adverse weather conditions, day or night, in conditions of dense countermeasures interference in regard to electronic warfare and direct fire from adversary air defence systems. As well as the strike mission the new aircraft design was to be capable of conducting a reconnaissance mission in which it would be a potential replacement for the Soviet/Russian fleet of Su-24MR tactical reconnaissance aircraft (UAC). Sukhoi describes the serial produced Su-34 as a 4th+ generation aircraft 'designed to deliver high-precision strikes on heavily defended air, ground and naval targets (including small and mobile targets) on solo and group missions in any weather conditions day or night, as well as for reconnaissance' (Sukhoi). The long operational range on integral fuel, and the availability of in-flight refuelling, allow the Su-34 to stretch the boundary definition of the tactical strike aircraft toward the intermediate range, although this should not cloud the fact that the Su-34 is a tactical strike fighter aircraft designed primarily as a Su-24 tactical strike aircraft replacement.

The Su-34 design had its genesis in the T-10V (T-10B) program, which had its genesis in the Sukhoi T-10UB program that produced the two seat Su-27UB (NATO reporting name 'Flanker C') as an operational conversion training aircraft to complement conversion training on the Su-27S (T-10S) (NATO reporting name 'Flanker B') air superiority fighter. Both the Su-27UB and Su-27S had their origins in the Sukhoi T-10 program developed as a 4th generation air superiority fighter through the 1970's (Sukhoi).

In the second decade of the twenty first century the Su-34 (top) design has established itself as the premier tactical strike aircraft in the Russian Aerospace Forces as a replacement for the Su-24M/M2 (top). UAC/Sukhoi

The T-10 program had commenced in 1969. Following several redesigns, the maiden flight of the T-10-1 was conducted on 20 May 1977 (pilot, V.S. Ilyushin) under the power of two A.M. Lyulka (now UEC Saturn) AL-21FZAI afterburning turbojet engines rated at 76.49 kN (~7800 kg) dry and 109.84 kN (~11201 kg) in afterburner (Sukhoi) – thrust may have been slightly in excess of these interim ratings. Several more T-10 aircraft followed – T-10-2, T-10-3 and T-10-4, the latter two being powered by two A.M. Lyulka (now UEC Saturn) AL-31F afterburning turbofan engines developed for the T-10 series production design. Each of these engines was rated at 79.43 kN (~8100 kg) dry and 122.59 kN (~12501 kg) with afterburner (Sukhoi). Following construction of the initial batch of four aircraft, a further five, T-10-5, T-10-6, T-10-9, T-10-10 and T-10-11, were built at the KnAAPO (Komsomolsk-on-Amur production plant). T-10 development aircraft were accepted for service testing in December 1979. Problems encountered during testing led to a redesign that resulted in the T-10S, to address issues, including controlling weight, reducing drag, increase wing lift and improving roll control. This was necessary as it had become clear that the desired superiority over its western counterparts, in particular the American McDonnell Douglas (now Boeing) F-15, could not be guaranteed with the original T-10 design. The incomplete T-10-7 development aircraft was completed as the prototype of the new design, receiving the designation T-10S-1. In this configuration the aircraft conducted its maiden flight on 20 April 1981 (pilot, V.S. Ilyushin), design leadership of the program passing to A.I. Knysheb that year (Sukhoi).

The Sukhoi T-10-1 during its maiden flight on 20 May 1977. Sukhoi

In the original T-10 design a major problem had been encountered with 'early stall on the wing', resulting in 'the sharp front edge of the profile along the entire span being subjected to shaking', which prohibited the successful execution of certain planned manoeuvres (TsAGI). To counter this, Sukhoi, acting on proposals forwarded by TsAGI (Central Aerodynamic Institute), decided to test, on the T-10S, a new wing of trapezoidal design 'with a root influx' and drooping, or deviating, wing tips (TsAGI). This translated to a new tapered wing with a straight, slatted leading edge flap, flaperon and cropped wingtips, incorporating wingtip missile launch stations that doubled as anti-flutter weights. The flaperons and differential tailerons replaced the ailerons of the original T-10 design. It was the changes to the fuselage that were most profound, with a shallower, longer, drooping nose and deeper spine. The twin vertical tail fin configuration of the T-10 was retained, but this was moved outboard from the original position on top of the engine nacelles to booms, which lay alongside the engines. The main undercarriage door mounted air brakes of the T-10 were replaced by a single spine mounted unit similar to that seen on the F-15. The new main undercarriage units were repositioned, as was the nose wheel undercarriage unit, which was moved slightly aft. However, even with the design changes incorporated, problems were encountered during flight testing, especially with the new wing design – a solution being found in reducing the wing area of the leading-edge slats (Sukhoi).

T-10-17, representative of the T-10S configuration, during testing in the early 1980's. Sukhoi

The T-10S (Su-27S) series production design would be powered by a pair of AL-31F turbofan engines first flown on the T-10-3. As serial production of the AL-31F commenced at A.M. Lyulka on 11 May 1984, early serial produced Su-27S were powered by development/pre-series production engines (Sukhoi). Available information indicates that the AL-31F has a nine-stage HP (High-Pressure) compressor, a four-stage LP (Low-Pressure) compressor and cooled single-stage HP and LP turbines to the rear of the combustor. The efficient air flow afforded by the combination of engine technology, aircraft air intake design and computer controlled variable inlet guide-vanes, contributed to the Su-27 high performance, conveying varying degrees of capability to conduct extreme high alpha manoeuvres, such as the 'Cobra' or 'Tail Slide', without the engines stalling (MMPP Salut & UEC Saturn).

The high thrust to weight ratio of the AL-31F bestowed upon the Su-27S a high maximum speed (Mach 2+), unrivalled (for the time) supersonic acceleration, climb rate, and manoeuvrability in certain flight regimes, such as sustained turn rate, for an aircraft in its class. Typical engine life was set at around 3,000 hours, a reasonable values for a Soviet era tactical combat aircraft engine. It should be noted that AL-31F engines have been run for thousands of hours over their scheduled life expectancy during bench test runs.

The serial Su-27S emerged with a length of 21.9 m, height, 5.9 m and wingspan, 14.7 m. Normal take-off weight was 23400 kg (Su-27SK) with 2 x R-27R1 (NATO reporting name AA-10 'Alamo'), 2 x R-73 (NATO reporting name AA-11 'Archer') air to air missiles and 5270 kg of internal fuel. Maximum take-off weight was set at 30450 kg (Su-27SK). The Su-27S/SK could accommodate 5270 kg of fuel at normal load and 9400 kg at maximum fuel-load. The huge volume of fuel allowed an impressive range to be attained – the Su-27S was capable of flying 1340 km at sea level armed with 2 x R-27R1 and 2 x R-73 missiles. In the same configuration, range was 3530 km at upper altitude (Sukhoi). Payload, which could be carried on ten wing and fuselage stations, was, according to Sukhoi data, 4430 kg (other sources suggest around 6000 kg), this being maximum with reduced fuel, while the 4430 kg stated by Sukhoi may be the maximum load carried with maximum fuel). Payload includes the primary armament of R-27 semi-active radar homing and infrared homing air to air missile variants and R-73 infrared guided air to air missiles as well as unguided air to surface munitions for the secondary air to surface role (Sukhoi).

A large, heavy air superiority fighter design, the Su-27S showed itself to have an exceptional performance in many areas, such as range, climb rate, manoeuvrability, in particular its high alpha flight performance, being superior to its rivals. The airframe has a +9 g overload limit that can be over-ridden by switching the limiter off (it should be noted that exceeding 9 g would be avoided except in emergency due to the adverse physiological effects of high g forces on a human. Maximum level speed is 1400 km/h at sea level and Mach 2.35 at upper altitude; climb rate, 19800 metres per minute at sea level and operational ceiling, 18500 m (Sukhoi).

The Su-27S would be equipped with a modern (for the 1980's) weapons system based around the RLPK-27 weapon control system. This featured a powerful N001 pulse-Doppler radar featuring a detection range of 150 km against a fighter size target (Tikhomirov). The radar complex was complemented by an electro-optical complex consisting of an OEPS-27 Electro-Optical Sighting System, an OLS-27 OLS (Optical Location Station) (Article 36Sh) – IRST (Infra-Red Search and Track) – and a LR (Laser Rangefinder), facilitating the detection, tracking and engagement of targets passively without the need for radar, the emissions of which betray the host aircraft position. The OLS was located forward of the windscreen, centred. A Shchel HPS (Helmet Pointing System), progenitor to the twenty first century HMTDS (Helmet Mounted Target Designation System), allowed engagements of off-boresight targets at angles of up to 60° by cueing sensors – the missile tracker head – onto targets.

When NATO aircraft began encountering the Su-27 from the mid-1980's it was noted that the aircraft carried new generation medium range air to air missiles, which emerged as the R-27 (P-27), which was serial produced in semi-active radar homing and infrared homing variants. US DoD

Once the design of the new air superiority fighter was finalised, the Su-27S entered series production and the first such aircraft, manufactured at Komsomolsk-on-Amur Aviation Plant, conducted its maiden flight on 1 June 1982 – conflicting Sukhoi documentation states the additional dates of 2 and 3 June 1982 – (pilot, A.N. Isakov, Sukhoi) (Sukhoi). State Joint Tests commenced on 10 August 1983 and stage LKI testing was completed on 21 August that year, with the full test series completed on 18 January 1984 (Sukhoi) – conflicting Sukhoi documentation states December 1983 as the completion date – which confirmed the designs expected flight performance superiority over its rivals. This paved the way for service entry, which occurred on 17 June 1985, with the 60th IAP-PVO FAR (Fighter Aircraft Regiment), although the first Su-27S did not actually arrive on 60th IAP-PVO FAR strength until 22 June that year (Sukhoi). Although having been in service for over five years the Su-27S was officially signed into service by a decree of the Soviet government, dated 23 August 1990 (confirmed in KnAAPO documentation, but conflicting PJSC Aviation Holding Company Sukhoi documentation states 26 August 1990) (Sukhoi). Following the introduction to service with the air forces of the Soviet Union in June 1985, Su-27 production continued, with in excess of 600 Su-27's produced through the Soviet Union dissolution into a Commonwealth of Independent States on 25 December 1991 and continuing into the early 1990's. Following the dissolution of the Soviet Union, the Su-27 remained in service in the new Russian state, assuming greater importance as older aircraft designs were retired. It is estimated that around 300 Su-27S remained in service in the Russia Federation in the mid-2010's. Smaller numbers of Su-27's equipped the air forces of some former Soviet Republics – the Republic of Belarus, Republic Kazakhstan, Ukraine and Uzbekistan – (NAZ) and new build aircraft were exported to China, Vietnam and Indonesia, while surplus aircraft were exported to several other nations (Sukhoi).

An S-27S of the Republic of Kazakhstan, armed with unguided rocket pods. Kazakhstan MOD

The basic Su-27S airframe spawned a number of variants, including the Su-27UB two-seat operational conversion trainer, which would form the basis for the initial design for a strike fighter variant of the Su-27. Development of the design that emerged as the Su-27UB had commenced in 1976 as the T-10U. The main external differences between the Serial Su-27S and the T-10U included redesigned forward fuselage in the latter, incorporating a second cockpit that was raised above the forward cockpit. This afforded an enhanced forward view for the occupant in the rear cockpit. A single piece canopy covers the two-place cockpit, with a one-piece windscreen ahead of the forward cockpit. The vertical tail planes and air brake were of increased height and area – the Su-27UB standing 500 mm taller than the Su-27S. Maximum take-off weight was increased from 30450 kg (Su-27S) to 33000 kg, which, along with aerodynamic changes resulting from the incorporation of the second cockpit, resulted in the overall performance being somewhat degraded compared to the Su-27S – maximum speed being reduced from Mach 2.35 to Mach 2.0 at altitude.

Range was also reduced from 1340 km (Su-27S) to 1270 km at sea level and from 3530 km (Su-27S) to 3000 km at upper altitude (Sukhoi). There was only a slight degradation in turn rates, initial climb rates and take-off and landing performance.

The Su-27UB operational conversion trainer introduced a second, slightly raised cockpit. Other than heightened tail fins, overall dimensions remained the same as those of the Su-27S, but maximum take-off weight was increased, which, combined with increased drag, slightly degraded overall performance. Author

The T-10U-1 (Su-27UB-1) conducted its maiden flight on 7 March 1985 (pilot, N.F. Sadovnikov) and State Joint Tests commenced on 24 May 1986 (Sukhoi). The Serial produced Su-27UB, the first of which conducted its maiden flight on 10 September 1986, was allocated the NATO reporting name 'Flanker C' – deliveries of serial production Su-27UB aircraft commenced in 1987 (Sukhoi).

Other derivatives of the Su-27 were under development in the late 1980's, including the T-10K (Su-27K) naval fighter – developed for operations from the Soviet Unions planned fleet of Project 1143.5 ACHC (Aircraft Carrying Heavy Cruiser) – and the T-10M (Su-27M) multifunction strike fighter. For the T-10K, T-10M and the planned T-10B, Sukhoi adopted what became known as the canard tri-plane configuration. This retained the rear all-moving horizontal tail planes, but added all-moving active canard fore-planes just ahead of the main wing where it joined the fuselage. The canard complex, design of which commenced in 1977, was studied as a means of increasing T-10 derivatives take-off and approach performance/characteristics and increasing manoeuvrability, this latter point being very much a secondary consideration (Sukhoi).

The T-10-24 canard triplane development aircraft (top) conducted its maiden flight in May 1985. The Su-27M (above) adopted the canard-triplane configuration, flying in this guise in 1988. Sukhoi

Prior to installation of the canard-triplane configuration on the T-10K/M/V, the canard configuration was tested on the T-10-24 development aircraft, the first T-10 variant to be equipped with canards, which conducted its maiden flight in May 1985 (Sukhoi).

Although initially associated with development of the T-10K, the prototype of which, T-10K-1, conducted its maiden flight on 17 August 1987 (pilot, V.G. Pugachev), the T-10M, the prototype of which conducted its maiden flight on 28 June 1988 (pilot, O.G. Choi), and T-10V, the T-10-24 was effectively used to prove the canard configuration for all canard tri-plane derivatives of the extended Su-27 family (Sukhoi). This included the Su-30MKI/SM and the Su-33KUB variants developed during the 1990's and into the twenty first century. All of the canard triplane configured T-10 derivatives, with the exception of the T-10K, were equipped with a digital-fly-by-wire flight control system.

The Su-27UB featured a second cockpit to undertake the operational conversion role whilst retaining combat capability of the Su-27S, albeit with a slight degradation in overall flight performance. The UB would eventually be developed into the Su-30 interceptor, which would form the basis of a plethora of multi-role Su-30MK variants. This Su-27UB is adorned with the colourful livery of the Russian Knights aerobatic display team. Sukhoi

In the early 1980's, as the Su-27S air superiority fighter was being developed, studies commenced into the feasibility of producing a two-seat strike variant of the design. This led to the Su-27IB (Istrebitel-Bombardirovshchik/fighter-bomber) program, the preliminary study phase of which was initiated in 1983. Initially, the Su-27IB strike fighter was designed around the Su-27UB two-seat operational conversion trainer airframe. Full scale development was formally authorised by a decree of the Soviet government dated 19 June 1986. The authorisation document called for the development of a two-seat 'fighter bomber' variant of the Su-27UB, the Sukhoi Design Bureau design code designation T-10B (T-10V) being applied around the same time (Sukhoi & UAC). Under chief designer Rolland G. Martirosov the design team drew up a draft of the T-10V design, which was conducted during the period 1987-1988 (Sukhoi & UAC).

The strike aircraft (fighter bomber) design, still with the tandem cockpit design associated with the Su-27UB layout, was subjected to a critical design review in May

1988, at which time proposals were put forward for an alternative side-by-side cockpit layout. The new design differed in many details to the previous incarnation. Most notably the aircraft was fitted with a distinctive enlarged nose section featuring the specified side-by-side seating for the two-crew – crew comfort being considerably enhanced over the previous generation Su-24M strike aircraft or the now defunct Su-27UB based strike aircraft design. The side-by-side crew arrangement offered many advantages over the tandem-cockpit layout. Notably it was far more spacious, the area behind the seats being spacious enough for the crew to stand up. A large windscreen and upper canopy were divided centrally. When the design was revealed it was initially thought by analysts that the canopy opened upwards in two-sections in a similar fashion to that seen on the Su-24 tactical strike aircraft. However, the T-10V canopy was fixed, entry to the crew cabin being through the nose wheel undercarriage bay via an integral ladder, which took the crew to the service hatch located on the rear wall of the cabin (Sukhoi). The bulky forward fuselage was built-up behind the cockpit area giving a hump back appearance. The LERX (Leading-Edge Root Extensions) were further forward than was the case with the Su-27UB, merging into the flattened nose section, which appeared chinned (Sukhoi). From a head-on aspect the flattened nose section was particularly distinctive, gaining the aircraft the nickname Platypus, after the flattened duck like bill of the Platypus (*Ornithorhynchus Anatinus*) egg-laying mammal indigenous to Australia. The forward fuselage shape and raised area to the rear of the cabin necessitated deletion of the spine mounted airbrake incorporated in the Su-27UB.

At the time of the design review in May 1988 the T-10V was specified to have high endurance on integral fuel with the ability to extend range through inflight refueling. The aircraft was to have high combat persistence and increased survivability over its predecessor, the Su-24M. The latter would be achieved through a number of design features – armoured cabin tolerant against low calibre explosive projectiles and a fuel tank system incorporating polyurethane foam filling (UAC).

As development work on the T-10V program ramped up in the late 1980's, following the design review of May 1988, it was decreed that mission capability would be facilitated through incorporation of an advanced avionics – incorporating multifunction indicator displays – and sensor suite, including high power multifunctional phased-array radar complex, an integrated optical-location complex and a high power EW (Electronic Warfare) complex (UAC). Although a similar program would emerge in the early 1990's under the Su-30MK designation, this would fall short of the strike/attack capability planned for the Soviet and later Russian Air Forces T-10V design. This would be required to have greater air to surface capability, advanced sensor suite optimised for the air to surface role and be capable of long-duration missions exceeding that intended for the Su-30MK series.

With the post design review alterations incorporated a single development prototype, T-10V-1, with the Soviet defence ministry designation Su-27IB, was ordered to be built at the Irkutsk production plant during 1989/1990. The T-10V-1 was little more than an aerodynamic prototype for the Su-27IB design, incorporating the canard-triplane layout. It was built from a series production Su-27UB with a new forward fuselage attached to the existing Su-27UB airframe forward of frame 18. The

T-10V-1 retained the extended height fins of the Su-27UB, but later aircraft would receive the smaller vertical tail associated with the Su-27S. The T-10V-1 omitted the ventral fins at the rear of the aircraft under the vertical tail fin fuselage area and incorporated a retractable inflight refueling probe positioned on the port side forward fuselage (Sukhoi) in line with the requirement to fly extended range missions. The twin nose-wheel unit was carried over from the Su-27K naval fighter. However, while the nose wheel unit retracted forward on Su-27S/UB and the Su-27K, it was retracted aft in the T-10V-1, with five separate doors covering the forward undercarriage bay. The T-10V-1's main undercarriage units, which retracted to lay in the wing fuselage joins, was reported as carried over from the Su-27K, but was actually more a standard Su-27UB undercarriage, strengthened to take the T-10V-1's increased weights.

An early application for the canard-triplane configuration beyond the T-10K, T-10M was the T-10V (T-10B), developed into the Su-34 multifunctional strike fighter. The T-10V-1 prototype, Blue 42, (top) conducted its maiden flight on 13 April 1990. Sukhoi

T-10V-1, which carried the side code Blue 42, conducted its maiden flight on 13 April 1990 (pilot, A.A. Ivanov, Sukhoi) (Sukhoi & UAC). In August 1990, western intelligence agencies received the first close look at the T-10V-1 when the aircraft was photographed by TASS news agency on a dummy approach to the new Soviet Project 1143.5 CTOL (Conventional Take-Off and Landing) ACHC (Aircraft Carrying Heavy Cruiser) *Tbilisi* (later renamed *Admiral of the Fleet of the Soviet Union, Kuznetsov* following the dissolution of the Soviet Union on 25 December 1991). It was immediately assumed by most western observers and analysts that the aircraft must be a two-seat conversion trainer for the naval T-10K (Su-27K). Whilst the T-

10V-1 was, like the T-10K, fitted with all-moving canards, even a cursory glance showed that it lacked the necessary naval equipment for aircraft carrier operations. Additionally, the aircraft lacked folding wings, although this in itself would not have precluded such an aircraft from operating from an aircraft carrier deck. The lack of other aircraft carrier operating equipment, such as an arrestor hook, would be contrary to that required for operations from an aircraft carrier deck. It was also unknown if the undercarriage had been strengthened to take the stress loads associated with high sink rate landings typical of aircraft carrier operations. The T10V-1 was not fitted with any under wing stores stations and wingtip stations were not active.

The illusion that the Su-27IB was a naval fighter conversion trainer was reinforced through interpretation/misinterpretation of a number of data sets. Information shows that the T-10V-1 was deployed to the AVMF (Soviet Naval Aviation) flight test centre at Novofyodorovka air base, at Saki on the Crimean Peninsula, during August 1990. As this was a naval flight-test centre, any news of this deployment would only reinforce the illusion that the aircraft was a naval strike fighter conversion trainer aircraft design. It is doubtful if the aircraft actually took-part in any real flight-testing at the centre other than demonstrations, with reports that the aircraft was summoned to the base by the then Soviet leader, Mikhail Gorbachev, whom apparently wished to inspect military hardware, including equipment being used in a Soviet Black Sea Fleet naval exercise, while he was in the Crimea. During the inspection the Soviet leader visited the *Tbilisi*, which was, at that time, undergoing sea trials following a number of modifications to the vessel. The aircraft complement apparently included three Su-27K naval fighters, at least one development Mikoyan MiG-29K naval fighter and several Kamov Ka-27 naval helicopters. Sukhoi flew a number of T-10V-1 demonstration flights, including simulated aircraft carrier approaches. A TASS photographer on-board the *Tbilisi* photographed the aircraft, resulting in the first photographs being released in the West giving the inference that the aircraft was landing on board the *Tbilisi*. What remains unclear is whether or not the release of the photographs was by chance of a TASS photographer being on-board or whether this was part of a Soviet plan of misinformation that prompted western intelligence agencies to infer that a naval aviation trainer rather than a strike aircraft was under development. In any event, western intelligence agencies and defence analysts appeared to more or less unquestionably accept that the aircraft was a naval trainer. This, despite a number of easily recognisable equipment omissions from the aircraft, which would have made it impossible to land on an aircraft carrier as noted above. Foremost among the omissions, as previously noted, was the lack of a naval arrestor hook, essential for conventional fixed wing operations from an aircraft carrier. When the lack of carrier operating equipment came to the fore it did not immediately kill-off the assumption that the aircraft was a naval trainer. Lack of naval systems meant very little other than that the aircraft would not land on the carrier during the demonstration. It would still have been possible for a proof of concept vehicle to fly dummy approaches in a similar fashion to that seen in the late 1980's with the French Dassault Rafale A concept demonstrator, which flew a number of aircraft carrier approach profiles with French Aircraft carriers even though it was deficient of naval equipment and was incapable of operating form the aircraft carrier deck. The most compelling evidence that the T-10V-1 was not the prototype of a naval operational conversion trainer was present in the fact that the Soviet Union was, at that time, developing the Sukhoi T-8UTG (Su-25UTG) as a conversion trainer for Soviet fixed wing aviation operating from the Project 1143.5 ACHC deck – the T-8UTG-1 (Su-25UTG-1) prototype had conducted its maiden flight on 1 September 1988 (Sukhoi).

Previous page: The T-10V-1 undertook a test/demonstration phase on approach to the Project 1143.5 Aircraft Carrying Heavy Cruiser *Tbilisi* (later *Admiral of the Fleet of the Soviet Union, Kuznetsov*) fuelling unfounded speculation that it was the prototype of a two-seat naval conversion trainer. This page: T-10V-1, in company with two Su-30 development/demonstration aircraft, refuels from a Soviet Ilyushin Il-78 airborne refuelling tanker aircraft. Sukhoi

Following release of the TASS photograph the western intelligence agencies assumption that the aircraft was a naval fighter trainer was not denied in the Soviet Union. The speculation of the new variants naval trainer role appeared to be warranted when it was reported, unofficially, that the aircraft was designated Su-27KU (Carrier Trainer) with a fallacious description of the design role – a two-seat trainer for carrier operations. The fact that side-by-side seating appeared to offer good visibility in the forward hemisphere when approaching the aircraft carrier deck, giving student and instructor a similar forward view, contributed to analysts inferring that the aircraft was indeed designed as an aircraft carrier capable conversion trainer. This can be considered Cold War misdirection on the part of the Soviets through non-denial of misinformed reports on the aircraft role facilitating the conditions for western intelligence agencies to accept such misinformation wholesale.

Having knowingly or unknowingly aided in the deception to the western intelligence agencies that the aircraft was a naval conversion trainer the TASS news agency was also responsible for revealing the aircraft's true identity and role. TASS released photographs of the aircraft carrying a number of air to air and air to surface weapon systems at the official unveiling of the T-10V (Su-27IB) during a display of the newest generation aircraft produced in the former Soviet Union, which took place at Machoolischchi air base, Minsk, on 13 February 1992 – the Soviet Union having been dissolved into a CIS (Commonwealth of Independent States). During this time of financial crisis in post-Soviet Russia, any hopes of sufficient state funding for accelerated development and production of new combat aircraft like the Su-27IB was not forthcoming. Therefore, many programs, including the Su-27IB, were left ticking along with no real prospect of sufficient near term state funding or orders from Russian or CIS air arms. The T-10V-1 made its public debut at the 1992 Mosaeroshow on 11 August 1992 (Sukhoi) and was demonstrated at MAKS 93 the following summer. The T-10V-1 continued flying in support of the Su-34 development program, contributing much, particularly in the areas of proving the basic aerodynamic concept.

T-10V development aircraft, T-10V-8, White 48, in formation with the Sukhoi T-50 (Su-57) development aircraft Blue 52 and a Sukhoi Su-35S development aircraft, circa 2013 – a portent to the near term future of Russian Federation tactical airpower. Sukhoi

The T-10V development program suffered inevitable delays attributed to both technical issues and, most seriously, the major funding shortfall within the Russian Federation. As the Russian government struggled under its post Communism financial crisis, aircraft manufacturers, along with other sectors, continued to suffer from chronic funding and order shortfalls. While the Su-34 program continued to receive drip funding, technical and financial problems severely delayed planned in-service dates. Due to the delays to the introduction of the new strike aircraft to service the Russian Air Force embarked upon a modest upgrade of its operational Su-24M 'Fencer' D fleet, extending the service life of this this design, designated Su-24M2.

2

T-10V DEVELOPMENT TO Su-34 SERIAL PRODUCTION

The T-10V-1 (T-10B-1), which was an aerodynamic test-bed for a strike fighter aircraft configuration, was followed by a number of development (pre-series production) T-10V aircraft built on a production line set up at NAPO (Novosibirsk Aviation Production Organisation), Novosibirsk (now NAZ (Novosibirsk Aviation Plant. V.P. Chkalova) branch of PJSC Sukhoi. The first pre-series T-10V, T-10V-2, White 43, conducted a 52 minute maiden flight from the Novosibirsk aviation plant on 18 December 1993 (crew, Igor V. Votintsev and Yevgeniy G. Revunov) (Sukhoi & NAZ) – UAC documentation states Votintsev and E.G. Howlers (UAC). T-10V-2, which was flown non-stop from Novosibirsk to Zhukovsky on 3 March 1994, where it was fully integrated into the flight test program, was followed by T-10V-5, White 45, which conducted its maiden flight on 28 December 1994. As more aircraft joined the development program flight testing increased, but at a slow pace due to funding constraints.

T-10V-5 was the first of the T-10V design to be shown in Western Europe when Sukhoi took the aircraft to Le Bourget airport, France, for the 41st Paris Air Salon in June 1995. The aircraft was entered in the salon with the service designation Su-32FN rather than Su-27IB previously associated with the T-10V program (Sukhoi). This resulted in confusion as the T-10V design was also being referred to as the Su-34. As the Su-32FN, the T-10V-5 was depicted as a maritime strike/anti-ship/ASW (Anti-Submarine Warfare) platform that could be equipped with a notional maritime optimised 'Sea Dragon' avionics/sensor suite. Equipment touted for this variant would have included a suite of expendable ASW sensors, which would have been housed in an under fuselage pod. However, in reality the aircraft differed little in detail from the T-10V-2 in regards to equipment fit.

When not masquerading as the Su-32FN at trade shows, T-10V-5 was involved in the T-10V trials program for clearance with the VKS (Russian Air Force). Reports of the aircraft flying evaluation missions during Russia's operations against insurgents in the Republic of Chechnya in 1999 have not been substantiated and should be discounted unless confirmation is forthcoming.

T-10V-5, White 45, adorned with the 349 exhibit code from its participation in the 42nd Paris Air Salon in June 1997. UAC

What Sukhoi described as the third (chronologically) series production Su-34, T-10V-4, White 44, conducted its 46 minute maiden flight from Novosibirsk on 25 December 1996 (Sukhoi). This aircraft was equipped with a full avionics/sensor suite (Sukhoi), but apparently lacked an EW (Electronic Warfare) suite, development of which had encountered delays. Following a short factory test phase T-10V-4 commenced flight-testing in earnest in early 1997. Contrary to fallacious reports that it was the T-10V-5 that was displayed at the 42nd Paris Air Salon in June 1997, it was actually T-10V-4. Unlike T-10V-5's appearance at Paris two-years previously, T-10V-4 participated in the flying program. On 8 August 1997, T-10V-4 was displayed at Kubinka Air Base, Russia, during the 50th anniversary celebrations of the 16th Air Army, which was followed by its display at MAKS 97, Zhukovsky. Moscow region, between 19 and 24 August that year. During this event T-10V-4 flew with weapon configurations, which included carriage of Kh-31 supersonic air to surface missile aerodynamic mock-ups.

It is thought that the T-10V-3 was a static test (non-flight) airframe, which would explain the out of sync side numbers of T-10V-1, White 42, T-10V-2, White 43 and T-10V-4, White 44. This is certainly a more rational explanation for the out of sync side numbers than some of the more outlandish theories of aircraft crashing and side numbers being changed to cover up the hypothesized crash, which is not backed up by evidence. It is known that at least one full-scale ground-test airframe was built. Static fatigue testing of the T-10V design was conducted at SIBNA (SIBNA), Sukhoi documentation showing that static testing of the design was completed on 26

November 1995 (Sukhoi). Ground test-rigs were built to test various systems for the design. GOSNIIAS conducted system tests on a T-10V HIL test-stand complex from 1987 through 1996 (GOSNIIAS).

Previous page top: T-10V-4 during low-speed handling trials. Previous page bottom: T-10V-5 depicted as the Su-32FN circa 1995. This page: Wearing the exhibit code 343 on the forward fuselage sides, the third T-10V development aircraft, T-10V-4, White 44, is towed from the static park at the Paris Air Salon in June 1997 (top) and taxiing for take-off at the start of its flight display (above). NAZ/Sukhoi/Author

T-10V-4 was utilised to clear the stores carriage options on the Su-34. The aircraft is here carrying aerodynamic mock-ups of **R-73E, R-27R1(ER1)** and **RVV-AE** air to air missiles and **Kh-31** series supersonic air to surface missiles. NAZ

T-10V-4 launching unguided rockets during trials. NAZ/Sukhoi

T-10V-5, White 45, taxiing to position for take-off at Farnborough International in September 2000. Author

T-10V-5, White 45, landing back at Farnborough in September 2000 following a demonstration flight. Author

T-10V static test airframe. SIBNA

The T-10V (Su-27IB) development program progressed painfully slowly during the 1990's. Joint State Tests of the Su-27IB (the program was being referred to under both the Su-27IB and Su-34 service designations) program commenced on 8 September 1996 (Sukhoi). A further two aircraft joined the development effort over the next several years – T-10V-6, White 46, conducted its maiden flight on 27 December 1997 and T-10V-7, White 47, conducted maiden flight on 21 December 2000 (Sukhoi).

Test were conducted with the 929th State Flight Test Centre at Akhtubinsk. A T-10V development aircraft participated in a military exercise at the Ashuluk military range in Russia in late 1999, the same year (28 July, 3 August and 19 August) that the T-10V design established seven T-10V aircraft class world records for carrying payloads to upper altitudes. World records held by the design include the following: An altitude of 14727 m attained when at a take-off weight of 36160 kg, including a 5000 kg payload, set on 28 July 1999; a time to height – 2000 m – with a 5130 kg payload, 28 July 1999; carrying a payload of 5000 kg to an altitude of 15063 m with the aircraft at a take-off weight of 34130 kg, 3 August 1999; record for carrying 5130 kg payload to specific altitude, 3 August 1999; carrying a 2300 kg payload to an altitude 16150 m, 19 August 1999; times for carrying a 1000 kg payload to an altitude of 16206 m and carrying a 2000 kg payload to an altitude of 16150 m, 19 August 1999. The three record flights on 19 August 1999 were flown by T-10V-5 during the MAKS 1999 trade show. A time to height world record was set, the aircraft attaining an altitude of 12 km in 58 seconds (UAC). Several more T-10V development aircraft, T-10V-8 to 10, were incorporated into the program in the early 2000's.

T-10V-6, White 46, during captive carry trials of external stores – R-73E short-range infrared guided air to air missiles on wingtip stations, RVV-AE medium range active radar guided air to air missiles on the outer wing stations, R-27R1/ER1 medium range semi-active radar guided air to air missiles on the intermediate wing stations, Kh-31 series supersonic air to surface missiles on the inner wing stations, R-27R1/ER1 missiles on the engine trunk stations and a KAB-1500 series 1500 kg class guided bomb unit on the fuselage centre station. UAC/Sukhoi

Top: T-10V-7, White 47, was employed as a weapons integration platform. The aircraft is configured with B8M1 rocket pods, each of which contain twenty S-80KOM/Ts-8BM unguided rockets, which can be launched singly or in salvo fire. Bottom: T-10V-7 landing configured with R-73E short-range infrared guided air to air missiles on the wingtip stations, R-27R1/ER1 medium range semi-active radar guided air to air missile on the intermediate wing stations, Kh-31 series supersonic air to surface missiles on the engine trunk stations and a single large air to surface store on the fuselage centre station. Sukhoi/NAZ

A T-10V development aircraft during a low altitude test flight. UAC

T-10V development aircraft during low altitude test flight(s). NAZ/UAC

Previous page: T-10V development aircraft, T-10V-8, White 48. This page: T-10V-8 (lower) in formation with a MiG-29K (Universal Family), MiG-35 (Universal Family), MiG-29OVT (research aircraft) and Su-35S multidimensional fighter. Sukhoi/NAZ

Three interrelated conditions enabled the continuation of the Su-34 program state tests in the period covering the late 1990's and early 2000's – a change of program personnel, including a change in general director at Sukhoi Design Bureau, a change in political leadership, and an upturn in the economic conditions prevailing in the Russian Federation as that state began to emerge from the economic downturn that preceded and followed the dissolution of the Soviet Union in December 1991. As well as advancement of the Su-34 program, Sukhoi pushed forward with updates of legacy Su-24M, Su-25SM and Su-27SM aircraft and continued to progress with advanced Su-27 derivatives – this eventually resulted in the $4^{th}++$ generation Su-35S, which flew for the first time in 2008 – and a 5th generation fighter aircraft design – this emerged as the Su-57 PAK FA (*Perspektivniy Aviacionniy Complex Frontovoi Aviacii* – Perspective Aviation Complex for Front line Aviation) that is scheduled to enter service in late 2019.

Going into the twenty first century increased funding enabled the development program to gather pace. By late 2002 the Russian Air Force was pushing for an accelerated introduction to service of a number of aircraft types, including the T-10V. The decision was taken to accelerate flight-testing, with more flights being conducted that year than had been conducted in the prior seven years of testing combined. By that time the Novosibirsk plant had completed ~eight airframes, with work continuing on another two – the development and integration of the AL-31F engines and airframe had been completed (Sukhoi). Much work remained to be conducted on the avionics/sensor and weapons systems intended for the serial T-10V, which, it had become clear, would be designated Su-34 in domestic Russian service, the Su-32 designation applying to export standard aircraft. The MODRF (Ministry of Defence of the Russian Federation) apparently approved serial production of the T-10V as the Su-34 multifunctional strike aircraft in March 2003, the Russian Air Force commander indicating that initial serial production would at least extend into double digits. However, further delays to serial production would emerge due to a number of considerations, not least of which was the implementation of a redesign of the avionics and cockpit ergonomics (Sukhoi) in light of advances in technology that had taken place whilst the T-10V program had been in a period of almost stagnation. In 2003, Sukhoi indicated that deliveries of serial produced Su-34 would commence around 2006 and initial production deliveries would extend into 2010, facilitated through funding allocated for the Russian weapon programs 2002-2010 (Sukhoi).

This unmarked aircraft adorned in factory primer is apparently the last of the T-10V development aircraft built to prove the designs flight and operational characteristics. Sukhoi

The first five serial production Su-34's were built at the NAPO Chkalov Aircraft Production Association plant in 2006-2008 (Kret). The first of these serial production machines, destined for the Russian Air Force, conducted its maiden flight from Novosibirsk and was delivered in 2006. Phase 1 of official state testing of the Su-34 was completed in October 2006, paving the way for Phase 2 testing, which the Sukhoi Aircraft Holding Company announced was underway on 12 December that year. Phase 2 testing, which would run for three years, included integration of new types of precision guided weapon options. When the first series production aircraft was delivered, the schedule (based on planned orders) called for 18 such aircraft to be delivered by 2010, with longer term plans for the construction of between 8 and ten aircraft per year. In 2008, a five year Russian Ministry of Defense contract called for the production of 32 Su-34's to be delivered during the period 2009-2013 (Sukhoi).

Under the Russian national defence order for 2009, two serial production Su-34's were delivered to the Russian Air Force on 21 December that year, increasing the pool of available aircraft for training/trials. Operational testing ramped up at the Russian Air Force test centre at Lipetsk, and Su-34's participated in the Russian military exercise Vostok 2010 (East 2010) in July 2010. The Su-34 design proved its long-range strike capability by flying non-stop from the European region of Russia to the Far East region of Russia where range targets were subsequently struck. The long-range mission was accomplished by utilising the aircrafts in-flight refueling capability – at least one in in-flight refueling being conducted. That same month, July 2010, Sukhoi announced that the Russian Air Force planned to replace 'virtually the entire fleet of Su-24 frontline bombers' then currently in service (Sukhoi). This indicated a long-term requirement for perhaps several hundred Su-34's. In March 2012 a contract was awarded, under the State Armament Program for 2011-2020 – production of 92 Su-34's would be undertaken at the Novosibirsk Aviation Plant (Sukhoi, NAZ & UAC). The 100th Su-34 was delivered on 19 August 2016 (Kret) with in excess of 120 having been ordered as of 2018.

Delivery of Su-34 Red 05 from Novosibirsk to the Russian Air Force on 21 December 2009. Sukhoi

Page 34 and page 35 top: Su-34 delivery to the Russian Air Force on 25 December 2012. Page 35 bottom: Su-34 assembly line at Novosibirsk. Sukhoi

Su-34 delivery to the Russian Air Force on 15 July 2013. Sukhoi

Sukhoi has produced conflicting dates in various documentation regarding completion of Joint State Tests – September 2011 and spring 2011 respectively (Sukhoi) whilst UAC (United Aircraft Corporation) documentation states such tests were completed in November 2010 (UAC). Completion of this phase paved the way for delivery of Su-34 serial aircraft to operational units, which commenced toward the end of 2011 – Su-34's participated in the Russian defence exercise Combat Commonwealth-2011 (Sukhoi). Five Su-34's were delivered from Novosibirsk to Voronezh air base in the Russian Western Military District on 25 December 2012 – December 2012 also saw the re-delivery of the final batch of upgraded Sukhoi Su-24M2 strike aircraft. Both types would form the backbone of the Russian Federation tactical strike aviation assets through the second decade of the twenty first century, which included extensive operational employment in support of the Syrian Arab Republics defence against ISIL (Islamic State of Iraq and the Levant), several other extremist organisations and western backed opposition groups. A further five Su-34's were transferred, under the 2012 state order, from Novosibirsk to Voronezh on 25 January 2013. The first Su-34 delivered under the 2013 state order was handed over to the Russian Air Force at Novosibirsk in May 2013, and three more were delivered in July that year, followed by deliveries in October and December 2013, which completed the 2008 order for 32 aircraft (Sukhoi).

The Su-34 was formally inducted into Russian Air Force service by a Russian Federation Government resolution dated 18 March 2014 (Sukhoi) or 20 March 2014 (UAC) – the discrepancy may well be the difference between documentation date and resolution implementation. On 10 June 2014, the first batch of Su-34's from the 2014 state defence order, part of the contract for 92 Su-34's awarded in 2012, was handed over to the Russian Air Force. This batch of Su-34's was delivered in a multi-tone aqua, with white nose cone and white vertical tail fin tops, colour scheme similar to that which adorned the pre-series and early production Su-34's.

Su-34

Page 37 and page 38 top: The first batch of Su-34 aircraft from the 2014 defence order was delivered to the Russian Air Force on 10 June 2014. Page 38 bottom: An Su-34 on delivery to the Russian Air Force on 15 October 2014. Sukhoi

Top: Su-34 on delivery to the Russian Air Force on 15 October 2014. Bottom: A Su-34 at a snowy Novosibirsk prior to a flight for delivery to the Russian Air Force on 27 November 2015. By this time the Su-34 was heavily engaged in flying operational bombing missions over the Syrian Arab Republic in support of the Syrian government forces operations against ISIL and other opposition groups in the Syrian civil war. Sukhoi

Su-34 delivery to the Russian Aerospace Forces in October 2015 (The Aerospace Forces, which incorporated the Russian Air Force, was formed on 1 August 2015. Sukhoi

Su-34

Page 41 top: One of four Su-34's delivered to the Russian Aerospace Forces mixed air regiment at Shagol air base, Chelyabinsk region of Russia on 17 December 2018. Page 41 bottom and page 42: Production of the Su-34 was ongoing in 2019. A Su-34 forward fuselage section on the Novosibirsk Aviation Plant assembly line (top) and an Su-34 being towed outside (above) on 23 August 2019. MODRF

Su-34 deliveries continued through 2016, including batches delivered to the Russian Air Force in August 2016, 31 October 2016 and 23 December 2016 – delivery of the latter batch fulfilling the 2016 State Defence Order. Deliveries continued through 2017, 2018 and 2019 (Sukhoi).

The Su-34 has established itself as the premier tactical strike aircraft in the inventory of the Russian Aerospace Forces, initially operating alongside upgraded Su-24M2 strike aircraft until sufficient numbers are available for the latter aircraft to be completely retired. With several hundred Su-24's remaining in Russian service it is doubtful if the type will be replaced one for one. Whatever the numbers produced, in the Su-34 the Russian Aerospace Forces possesses a highly capable $4^{th}+$ generation tactical strike aircraft capable of striking targets at not only tactical, but close to intermediate ranges, with precision guided or unguided weapons. As well as deliveries of the Su-34, the Russian Aerospace Forces, resurgent following the painful years of drawdown and funding shortages following the dissolution of the Soviet Union in December 1991, is also, in the second decade of the twenty first century, receiving other advanced combat aircraft designs – $4^{th}+$ generation Sukhoi Su-30SM multifunctional fighter, $4^{th}++$ generation Su-35S multidimensional fighter and 5th generation Su-57 multidimensional fighter.

3

SU-34 FULLBACK

Design features of the serial produced two crew Sukhoi Su-34, allocated the NATO (North Atlantic Treaty Organisation) reporting name 'Fullback', include retention of the canard-tri-plane layout – incorporation of canard foreplanes improved stability of flight at all operating altitude and speeds regimes – two high power afterburning turbofan engines, the ability to carry a large payload of guided and or unguided air to air and air to surface weapons, the ability to strike surface targets at ranges beyond that previously attainable by tactical combat aircraft on integral fuel, the ability to refuel inflight, increased autonomous operation capability, increased survivability for crew and aircraft, advanced sensor suite and open architecture avionics to ease incorporation of updates as technology advances became available (Sukhoi).

Whereas the previous generation Sukhoi Su-24M series had a limited self-defence capability with short range infrared guided air to air missiles, the Su-34 would feature an advanced capability to employ medium range semi-active radar guided, active radar guided and potentially medium range infrared guided air to air missiles as well as short range infrared guided weapons. While the Su-34 air to air capability would fall short of that attained by the $4^{th}++$ generation Su-35S developed as an Su-27S replacement within the Russian Federation Air Force (Aerospace Forces from 1 August 2015), it was developed to be in advance of that of 4th generation and some $4^{th}+$ generation tactical fighter aircraft designs, provisioning a capability to operate in airspace contested by an opponent's air defence aircraft with greater confidence of mission fulfillment.

The basic design characteristics of the Su-34 include, length, 23.34 m; height, 6.09 m; main wingspan, 14.7 m; wing area, 62 m^2 and normal take-off weight, 38240 kg. Maximum range at sea level when configured with 6 x FAB-500 bombs, 2 x R-73E short range air to air missiles, 2 x RVV-AE medium range air to air missiles and three PTB-3000 external fuel tanks, is put at 1750 km, extending to 3000 km at upper altitude. Operational radius at low altitude, approaching sea level, with maximum internal fuel load, is 1100-1130 km (this can vary depending on aircraft stores load). Ferry range is 4000 km; maximum airborne time, 10 hours (crew dependent);

maximum flight speed at upper altitude, 1900 km/h (1,181 mph) without external stores; maximum speed at low altitude, approaching sea level, 1300 km/h without external stores (conflicting Sukhoi documentation states 1400 km/h); maximum Mach number, 1.6; operating ceiling without external stores, 15000-17000 m; take-off run, 750 m; landing run with brake parachute deployed, 1000 m (Sukhoi & UAC).

Russian Air Force (Aerospace Forces) Su-34, Red 38. Rosoboronexport

The Su-34's outstanding flight performance, including a high level of manoeuvrability, is facilitated by a number of design traits, including the highly efficient aerodynamic layout, high power engines and fly-by-wire flight control system (Sukhoi). The Su-34 retains the distinctive blended wing body layout demonstrated in the Su-27S/UB. The Su-34 design, which utilises advanced materials, CFC (Carbon Fibre Composites), in some areas of its construction, such as new undercarriage doors, is not a true stealth driven aircraft design, although like other $4^{th}/4^{th}+$ generation tactical combat aircraft, reduced RCS (Radar Cross Section) measures have been incorporated into the design. The Su-34 design includes sharp edged chines on the forward nose section, which blend rearward to the LERX's (Leading-Edge Root Extensions), giving a blended wing body appearance, which contributes to reducing the radar signature. A number of other RCS reduction measures have been taken, these possibly including the addition of radar absorbent materials on the airframe (unconfirmed). While it is clear that the Su-34 has a lower RCS compared to previous generation tactical strike aircraft, including the Sukhoi Su-24 and European Panavia Tornado, it is also claimed that the RCS is lower than its nearest American analogue, the Boeing F-15E Eagle (Strike Eagle) (unconfirmed). According to the design team, the RCS of the Su-34 is around the same as that of a modern cruise missile (Sukhoi).

The canard-triplane layout adopted for the T-10V design, demonstrated here on Su-34, Red 38, improved stability of flight at all operating altitudes and speed regimes. UAC

Head-on views of the Su-34 during ground taxiing operations, highlighting the flattened appearance of the forward fuselage to the fore of the crew cabin. UAC/NAZ

Su-34

Page 47-48: The Su-34 retained much of the aerodynamic layout and qualities of the Su-27S/UB from which it was developed. UAC/Sukhoi/Kret

Su-32 export standard three view general arrangement drawing, relevant to the Su-34. NAZ

Main external differences between the T-10V-1 and subsequent T-10V (Su-34) aircraft included the latter having a larger hump aft of the cabin, an enlarged tail boom, more pronounced protruding edge at the wing-root extension, shorter tail fins of the Su-27S and Su-27K instead of the taller vertical tails of the Su-27UB incorporated in the T-10V-1, and a stronger undercarriage complex of twin main-wheel units, which replaced the Su-27UB type single main wheel undercarriage units incorporated in the design of the T-10V-1 (Sukhoi). The new twin-main-wheel undercarriage complex was designed with the wheel units arranged in tandem to better distribute the increased weight of the Su-34, increasing the aircraft's ability to operate at higher operating weights and in poorly developed off-base locations. When retracted, the main wheel units rotate ~90° and are housed horizontally in the wing/fuselage root. The forward twin nose wheel unit, which is adapted from the twin wheel unit incorporated in the Su-27M design, retracts aft to lay in the forward fuselage.

The Su-34 features an undercarriage complex of twin tandem main-wheel units (top) and a forward twin nose wheel unit (top and above). NAZ/UAC

Su-34 Red 21, Red 20 and several unidentified aircraft (top) and Red 22 (above) at dispersal at an undisclosed air base within the Russian Federation. UAC

Operating in much of Russia's vast territorial expanse, from the Arctic North through the hinterland to the South, from West to East, is all too often conducted in conditions of snow and ice. The Su-34 undercarriage system is designed to facilitate efficient operation in such environmental conditions. UAC/Sukhoi

The Su-34 is equipped with a brake parachute that deploys on touch down reducing the overall landing run required. This is employed in base operations (top) and in off base operations. Russian Aerospace Forces Su-34 units practice off base operations. This grouping of aircraft are dispersed in a roadside parking area during an off base training exercise, whereby the aircraft operated from strips of highway, in August 2019. MODRF

MODRF Russian language graphic outlining a number of basic design characteristics of the Su-34. The main points of the text are reproduced below in English.

Crew: 2

Crew members can stand upright in the cockpit, which allows them to restore working ability [such as relaxing] stiff muscles. There is a toilet and a closet in the cabin for heating food. All this provides high performance of pilots in the long (up to 10 hours) duration flight.

Maximum take-off weight: 44360 kg
Length: 23.3 m
Wingspan: 14.7 m
Wing area: 62 m^2

Maximum speed: 1900 km/h
Flight range: 4000 km
Combat radius: 1100 km
Practical ceiling: 17000 m (this is 2000 m higher than the 15000 m value provided by Sukhoi. The lower value may refer to that intended for the Su-32 export standard)
External stores load: 8000 kg

Su-34

Previous page: Forward and rotated views of a 3-D digital rendering of the Su-34 external layout. This page: Plan view of the Su-34 depicted in Russian Aerospace Forces scheme. MODRF/UAC

Top: Infographic depicting several technical and flight characteristics of the Su-34. Above: AL-31F turbofan engine, similar to the series 23 installed in the Su-34. UAC/Author

The high power turbofan engines provision for the Su-34 to conduct aggressive manoeuvres at all flight altitudes. UAC

Top: Vapour streams from the upper surfaces of a Su-34 as it maneuvers during a demonstration flight. Above: The aerodynamic design of the Su-34 air intakes provision for adequate air to reach the engines even when the aircraft is maneuvered at high angles of attack. GosMKB Vympel /UAC

Ghosted graphic showing the internal layout of the Su-34 engine bays. Note the T-10V-1 type undercarriage. UAC

Sukhoi documentation shows that the Su-34 is powered by the AL-31F Series 23 afterburning turbofan engine – UAC documentation refers to the engine variant powering the Su-34 as the AL-31FM (UAC). As noted above, the AL-31F powering the Su-27S and Su-27UB had a thrust rating of 79.43 kN in military power (dry) and 122.59 kN with afterburner (Sukhoi). According to information released by PJSC Sukhoi, the Series 23 engine has the same basic thrust ratings as those applied to the baseline AL-31F (Sukhoi). As previously noted, available information states that the standard AL-31F that powered the Su-27S/UB has a nine-stage HP (High-Pressure) compressor, a four-stage LP (Low-Pressure) compressor and cooled single-stage HP and LP turbines to the rear of the combustor. The engines are widely spaced in all Su-27 derivatives, including the Su-34, allowing the carriage of external stores between the engine nacelles. While this was typically R-27R1(ER1) medium range air to air missiles in the Su-27S air superiority fighter, the Su-34 can accommodate a diversity of guided and unguided air to surface stores – ranging from KAB-1500 1500 kg class guided bomb units to FAB-500 500 kg class unguided bomb units. The Su-34 can also accommodate a PTB-3000 (3050 litre) external fuel tank on the centre line stores station between the engine bays. The wide spacing of the engines add to aircraft safety and survivability by reducing the chances of both engines being lost if one engine is damaged. Typical engine life is set at around 3000 hours.

The excellent air flow afforded by the combination of engine technology, the Su-34 intake design and computer controlled variable inlet guide-vanes, contribute to the Su-34 designs excellent flight performance, conveying varying degrees of high alpha manoeuvres without the engines stalling. This capability, although exceptional for an aircraft in its weight class, falls short of that attained by the Su-27S air superiority, Su-30SM multifunctional or Su-35S multidimensional fighter aircraft.

AL-41F afterburning turbofan engine. UMPO

At the higher operating weights of the Su-34, it was clear that the design would benefit from application of a higher performing engine. There were several options for provisioning a more capable engine for the Su-34. One such option studied was the AL-31F-1M, developed by FSUE Gas Turbine Engineering MMPP Salut (MMPP Salut), introduced on the second contract for upgrades of the Su-27S to Su-27SM standard and installed in the Su-27SM3 new build aircraft. The AL-31F-1M (Series 42) engine, has an afterburning rating of 13500 kgf – later MMPP documentation suggests a rating of 14500 kgf (MMPP Salut).

It has was hypothesised over several years that the NPO Saturn AL-41F (117S) afterburning turbofan engine, which powered Su-35S 4th++ generation and development examples of the Su-57 5th generation multidimensional fighter aircraft designs, could be installed in the Su-34 – this being formalized in 2019 for aircraft in service with the Russian Aerospace Forces, but no timetable for implementation of the engines into the fleet was released.

The AL-41F (117S) engine, developed by UEC Saturn Research and Production Association, is a radically modified derivative of the AL-31F. Production of the engine is a co-operative venture between UMPO (Ufa Motor Building Association) and Rybinsk based UEC Saturn, both incorporated within United Engine Corporation. Although not referred to as such in UEC Saturn documentation, the 117S is confirmed by United Aircraft Corporation and UMPO as carrying the designation AL-41F-1S. The 117S incorporates many 5th generation design features, including a new fan design, new high and low pressure turbine designs and a new digital control system. Available thrust, at 14500 kgf in afterburner mode, is increased by around 16% over that of the AL-31F (UEC Saturn). This, however, would suggests a higher thrust for the AL-31F than the values released.

Su-34 engine bay fuselage section on the NAZ assembly line in August 2019. MODRF

The by-pass engines form the core of the power plant complex that includes a fire extinguisher, engine management and control system, auxiliary turbine, auxiliary gearbox and an inlet control system (UMPO, UEC Saturn & Sukhoi).

The Su-34 internal fuel capacity is 11400 kg (this value refers to the Su-32, the inference of data provided in some Sukhoi documentation being that this applies also to the Su-34, but contradictory documentation from Sukhoi puts forward a value of 12100 kg, although this appears to have been superseded by the lower value). Fuel capacity can be increased through the carriage of up to three PTB-3000 3050 litre capacity external fuel tanks. Maximum flight range, when configured with 6 x FAB-500 bombs, 2 x R-73E missiles, 2 x RVV-AE missiles and three x PTB-3000 external fuel tanks, is put at 1750 km, when operating at sea level, and 3000 km at upper altitude. Range can be significantly extended through the incorporation of an in-flight refuelling complex. This is centred on a retractable refuelling probe (apparently a GPT-2E series nozzle assembly) located on the port side forward fuselage, and a fuel inlet capable of operating at an air inlet pressure of 3.5 kg/cm^2 (1100 l/m) (Sukhoi & UAC). The inflight refueling probe allows the Su-34 to refuel in flight from airborne tanker aircraft – Ilyushin Il-78M with UPAZ-1 pod – or from tactical combat aircraft equipped with a UPAZ in-flight refuelling pod. Aircraft survivability is increased through measures to render the fuel tanks and bays explosion proof (certainly reducing the likelihood of explosion) through polyurethane filling of fuel tanks (UAC).

Su-34, Red 10 (top) and Red 11 (bottom), configured with a single PTB-3000 external fuel tank on the fuselage centre station. Sukhoi/UAC

Su-34, Red 21 (top) and Red 11 (bottom), configured with PTB-3000 external fuel tanks on the fuselage station. UAC

Top: The Su-34 retractable inflight refuelling probe in the closed position on T-10V-4 development aircraft White 44. Above: Su-34 Red 11 approaches the boom of a UPAZ-1 pod of an Il-78M tanker aircraft on 9 February 2019. Author/MODRF

Top: Su-34, Red 11, approaches the boom to refuel from a UPAZ-1 pod of an Il-78M inflight refuelling tanker aircraft on 6 July 2019. Above: Su-34 tail boom section in the NAZ assembly hall in August 2019. MODRF

One of the most readily distinguishable features between the T-10V-1 and later T-10V aircraft is the enlarged and elongated rear tail boom of the Su-34 pre-series and series production standard aircraft. Sukhoi had demonstrated a larger tail boom on the experimental T-10-20 (the T-10-20R) modified for an attempt on the world speed record over a closed circuit distance of 500 km. The longer tail boom was utilised to house an additional fuel tank required for the record attempt to be conducted at sustained supersonic speeds, which would consume fuel at a prodigious rate. The aircraft was never used to conduct the record attempt and was eventually retired and placed as a museum exhibit.

When it first emerged publicly in the early 1990's, the enlarged tail boom of the T-10V series that followed T-10V-1, was wrongly assumed to be the housing for a rear facing search radar. The true function of the boom is a platform for an internal fuel tank, an APU (Auxiliary Power Unit), self-defence electronic warfare chaff dispenser and the landing brake parachute system on the fore section of the boom upper surface – as is the case with the Su-35S, the parachute box, located on top of the boom, pops-up prior to chute deployment. The TA-14-130-35 APU (specified for the Su-32), developed by JSC NPP Aerosilia, provisions for increased ability to conduct off-base operations without recourse to ground based power supply (Sukhoi).

The Su-34 tail boom houses an internal fuel tank, the TA-14-130-35 APU, elements of the self defence suite and the landing brake parachute complex. Author

On side-on view the extended length tail boom of the Su-34 takes on the appearance of a most prominent feature of the aircraft rear section. UAC

The Su-34 is equipped with a twin-canopy brake parachute complex that pops up from the housing toward the forward section of the extended tail boom before deploying into the slipstream and opening. UAC

The Su-34 is equipped with a digital quadruple redundant FBW (Fly by Wire) FCS (Flight Control System). This may be developed from the MNPK Avionica (now JSC Moscow Scientific-Production Complex 'Avionics') FBW FCS developed for the Su-27M in the late 1980's and early 1990's (unconfirmed). In the Su-27M, this system featured four longitudinal channels in pitch and three transverse channels in roll/yaw – the first generation Su-27S featured FBW in pitch only. The channel for control of the canard foreplanes also functioned as a redundant channel.

The combination of aerodynamic shaping, high power engines and FBW FCS bestow upon the Su-34 a level of maneuverability unprecedented for an aircraft in its class – the Su-34 is credited with an overload limit of +9 g whilst the export standard Su-32 is credited with an overload limit of +7.5 g (Sukhoi & UAC). Conflicting Sukhoi documentation states +8 g overload limit for the Su-34 (Sukhoi). The Su-34 is able to conduct aggressive manoeuvres, even at at ultra-low-altitudes – the Su-34 can fly at low flight altitudes in 'by-pass and fly-by' modes (Sukhoi) increasing flight comfort, even in environmental conditions pertaining to turbulence. This combination of factors reduces crew fatigue and aids in overall mission effectiveness, allowing increased duration missions to be undertaken. The Su-34 incorporates an active-safety system, which itself incorporates artificial intelligence into some elements of operation. The system, in combination with onboard computers, allows the Su-34 to deliver simultaneous precision strikes against several surface targets whilst the aircraft is being actively maneuvered to avoid threats at upper and lower altitudes, a terrain following mode being incorporated for operations in the latter flight environment (Sukhoi).

Su-34 multifunctional strike fighters break port and starboard at low altitude. Sukhoi

A Su-34 pulls up almost to the vertical, demonstrating the types capability to perform such extreme manoeuvres, approaching that of its lighter air superiority lineage – the Su-27S. UAC

The Design of the Su-34 advocated a significant increase in aircraft survivability over its predecessor, the Su-24. Designed when low-altitude strike scenarios were considered the best option for aircraft survival, the Su-34 features an armoured crew cabin, described as a 'titanium armoured capsule' (Sukhoi). This increases crew protection at all altitudes, but most notably at lower altitudes where the aircraft may encounter small calibre ground fire and MANPADS (Man Portable Air Defence Systems) – typically short-range infrared guided SAM (Surface to Air Missiles). In all conflicts, since the Gulf War of 1991, in which NATO and NATO affiliated nations have been involved, the emphasis has been on medium altitude operations as this increases the aircraft survivability by operating above most anti-aircraft fire and MANPADS. It should be noted that all of these conflicts, through 2019, have been conducted against opponents operating obsolete air defence systems or, indeed, having no air defence capability at all. On the few occasions in which US (United States) of America Patriot surface to air missiles engaged US and British aircraft in so called friendly fire incidents over Iraq in 2003, the aircraft were destroyed, indicating the poor survivability of modern aircraft if confronted by a modern air defence system at medium altitudes. The Russian aerospace doctrine accepts the lethality of advanced air defence systems, with tacit acknowledgment that in a large scale conflict in Europe, aircraft survivability would be increased at low altitudes.

The two crew of the Su-34 are accommodated in a spacious armoured cabin, referred to as a titanium alloy capsule. This affords the crew protection from small arms and small calibre anti-aircraft weapons, as well as blast fragments from exploding missile warheads. UAC

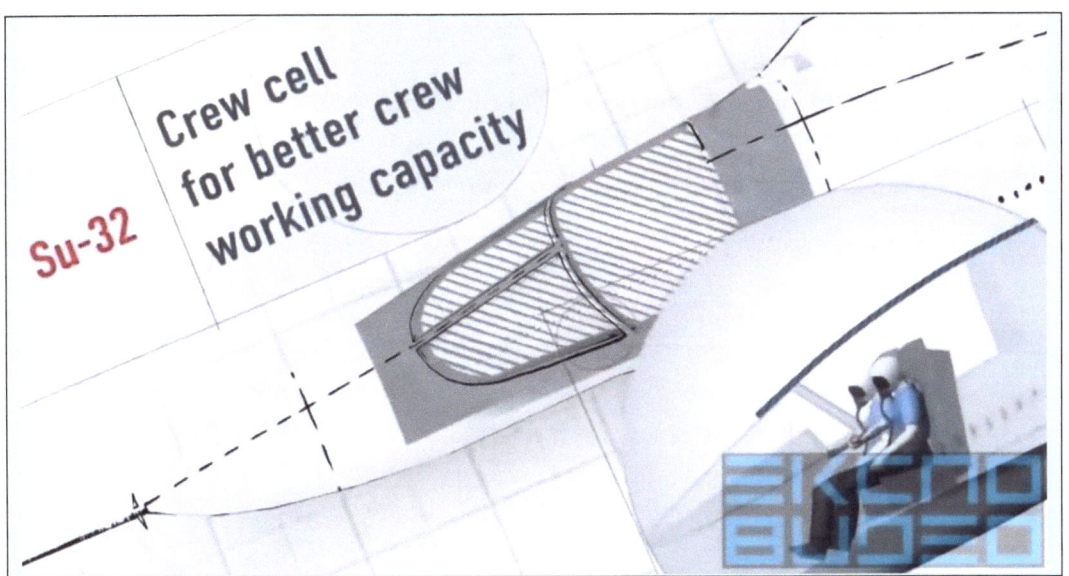

Top: Still graphic showing the armoured capsule concept of the export standard Su-32, which is representative of the Su-34. Above: The Su-34 crew are seated side-by-side in a spacious cabin, which has standing room at the rear. UAC & MODRF

In a departure from the tight fit cockpit of previous generation tactical combat aircraft, the Su-34 crew of two – pilot and navigator/WSO (Weapon Systems Operator) – benefit from a spacious cabin that actually caters for a person to stand at full height at the cabin rear. Access to the crew cabin is via an integral fixed ladder within the forward fuselage undercarriage bay. The enhanced crew conditions, compared to previous generation tactical combat aircraft, facilitates a doctrine for operations of up to ten hours duration (UAC). The cabin canopy is fixed and does not open for crew access.

Integral ladder of the forward fuselage undercarriage bay for access to the Su-34 crew cabin. Sukhoi

The two crew are seated on K-36D-3.5 zero zero ejection seats positioned side-by-side in the armoured cabin (Sukhoi & UAC) – the export standard Su-32 has been specified with the K-36D-3.5E – development of which was completed in 2001. The ejection seat is designed to afford protection for the occupant against 'dynamic pressure G-loads' during the ejection sequence through incorporation of 'protection gear, windblast shield, forced restraint in the seat, seat stabilization' and the ability to select from three operation modes that would be dependent on occupant mass (NPP Zvezda). Following ejection, the occupant separates from the seat and a descent parachute deploys. The escape system, of which the K-36D-3.5 seat is the major element, incorporates a KKO-15 complex consisting of oxygen equipment and various protection equipment. The seat complex also incorporates a survival kit, which detaches from the seat along with the occupant for the descent phase. A life raft is incorporated to provide flotation for the occupant in the event of a landing on water – the weight of the seat and survival kit is around 103 kg (NPP Zvezda).

The major aircraft operating parameters in which the seat can be safely deployed includes a host platform speed of 0-1300 km/h, with absolute speed range up to Mach 2.5, and altitudes from 0-20000 m, considerably in excess of the operating parameters of the Su-34 (NPP Zvezda).

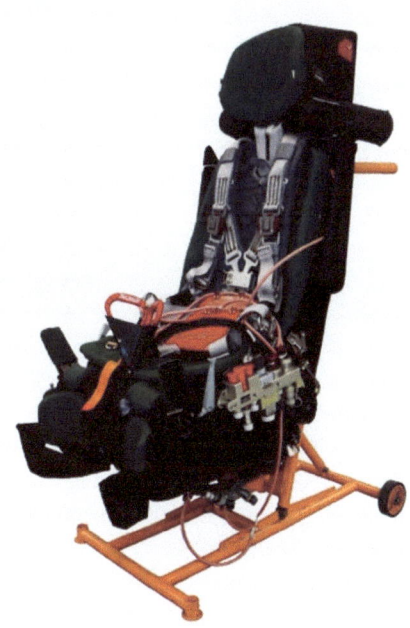

Above: The Su-34 is equipped with Zvezda K-36D-3.5 zero zero ejection seats – the export standard Su-32 would be equipped with K-36D-3.5E ejection seats. NPP Zvezda

The life-support system includes the KDA-15 oxygen system to provide the crew with oxygen at altitudes up to the aircraft maximum operating altitude (Kret). This can be substituted with a KC-129 complex, which supplies both crew with oxygen for operations at altitudes up to 20000 m, in excess of the operating ceiling of the Su-34. Oxygen is generated from compressed air taken from the gas turbine compressor. This means there is no requirement for on-board oxygen cylinders, reducing the pre-flight preparation requirements with the added benefit that mission duration is not limited due to oxygen cylinder supply (NPP Zvezda).

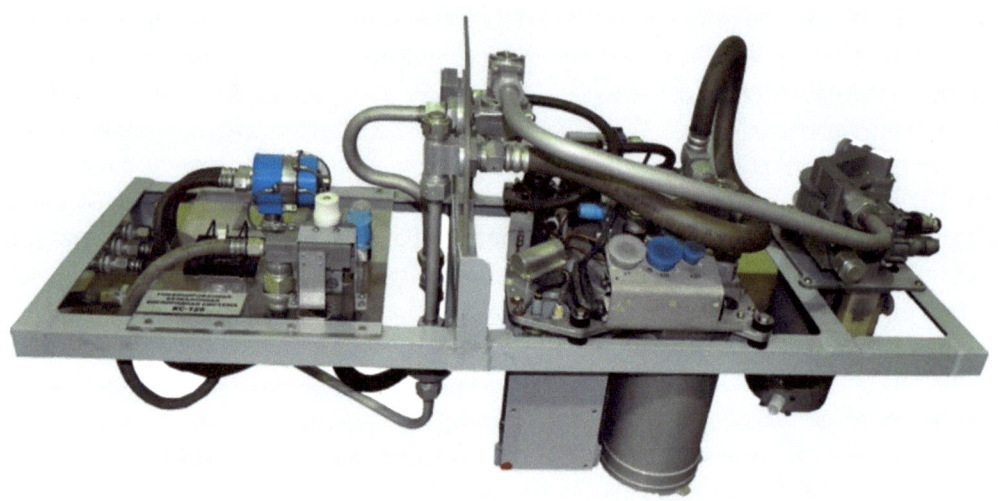

The onboard oxygen complex supplies crew with oxygen for operations up to an altitude of 20000 m, in excess of the operating ceiling of the aircraft. NPP Zvezda

Modern sensors/avionics would be fundamentally essential to arriving at a weapon system with capabilities significantly in advance of previous generation strike aircraft. On the basis of this requirement the Su-34 would be the first Russian combat aircraft design to feature an open-architecture avionics complex, allowing the addition or update of equipment without the need for a fully comprehensive replacement of onboard systems (Sukhoi).

The cabin features a modern glass control panel that incorporates five MFI-66 colour multifunction display screens and a KAI-1-01 (specified for the Su-32) collimator (HUD (Heads up Display)). Each MFI-66 display complex features a series of push buttons to allow easy access to various data formats for the display of relevant system and operational data, such as flight parameters and aircraft status – fuel, weapons etc. – to the crew. The Su-34 retains a mechanical back-up facility, which can duplicate flight information in the event of primary system failure(s) (Sukhoi). Flight and navigational data, as well targeting data, is displayed on the KAI-1-01 collimator at head height. The domestic Su-34 is equipped with a digital HUD-31M collimator (HUD) (Electroautomatics), an advancement of the analogue ILS-31 previously specified for development T-10V aircraft. Crew situational awareness is amplified by the incorporation of a voice warning system, which can provide alerts to potential hazards (Sukhoi).

The Su-34 cockpit section of the flight cabin is dominated by five MFI-66 colour multifunction display screens and a single collimator (HUD) for the pilot on the port side. MODRF

The other major information source available for the Su-32 would be a HMTDS (Helmet Mounted Targeting Designation System) of the NSTS-T/TE type, which would display tactical information and facilitate the cueing of weapons for engagement of airborne or surface targets through movement of the pilots or WSO head through receipt of data obtained by head pointing the sensors – within line of sight. The NSTS-T features operating angles of azimuth ± 60° and elevation +60° to -15°, with a maximum targeting error of 40 arcminutes (Electroautomatics).

Graphic still showing the location of the Sh-141-02E radar in the Su-32 and demonstrating the complexes ability to search, track and target airborne and ground targets. UAC

The onboard sensor suite consists of an advanced multifunctional electronically scanned radio-electronic passive PAA (Phased Array Antenna) complex, an optoelectronic complex and an electronic warfare system, built around the Sh-141-02 radar, Platan laser television sighting station and the L-175V radio electronic warfare complex (anti-radar). The frontal aspect Sh-141-02E, developed by JSC TsNPO Leninets, from work conducted on the bureau's V-004 passive phased-array radar that commenced flight testing in 1997, is an advanced multifunctional radar complex with an advanced phased-array antenna. No detailed performance data has been released for the Sh-141-02, but the Sh-141-02E, specified for the export standard Su-32, can detect a fighter size airborne target at ranges out to 120 km at viewing angles form the aircraft frontal aspect of ±60° (Sukhoi). UAC states that the complex can identify airborne targets at distances out to 250 km (UAC), this performance trait apparently referring to the Sh-141-02 equipping Su-34 in domestic Russian service. Ten airborne targets can be tracked, four of which can be engaged simultaneously with the aircraft's air to air armament. In the air to surface mode the Sh-141-02E complex can detect a large target, such as a bridge, at ranges out to 100 km. In the air to surface mode four targets can be tracked and engaged simultaneously. Other air to surface modes include high resolution mapping of the Earth's surface (Sukhoi).

The 623-3DR aircraft radar interrogator, which has a range of up to 200 km against airborne targets and up to 300 km against sea surface targets, has been specified for the Su-34 (Kret), but the status of is integration as of 2019 is unclear. A variant of the Hunter multifunction image processing system, known as Sycamore, was cleared for installation on the Su-34. Hunter systems are designed to automatically detect, in the sensors field of view, easing process detection and auto tracking of targets (Kret).

Top: The Sh-141-02/E was developed from the Leninets V-004 passive phased-array radar. Above: The quasi-oval shaping of the radar phased-array antenna was a consequence of the flattened nose design of the T-10V design. UAC/Author

The Platan laser television sighting station, developed by JSC UMOZ PO, is housed on the Su-34 fuselage underside. This complex can survey the Earth surface and guide, through incorporated laser and television channels, laser and television guided weapons, as well as provide targeting data for accurate delivery of unguided weapons – bombs and rockets. The complex provides for a search mode and recognition of surface features, which are replicated as television imagery to the navigator/WSO on the onboard MFI-66 display screen(s). Surface targets, stationary or moving, can be tracked with a television image replicated on the display screen(s). The laser can measure range to targets and illuminate surface targets when employing laser guided ordnance against same (Sukhoi).

What is termed 'an intelligent radar counteraction and defence system' (UAC) as part of the Su-34 sensor suite refers to the L-175V (L-175B) Khibiny electronic warfare complex (L-175VE specified for the Su-32), which is confirmed as the major element of the onboard electronic warfare suite (Sukhoi, UAC & KNIRTI). This system, developed by JSC Kaluga Research Radio Engineering Institute, is capable of providing electronic warfare protection, countering radar, sonar and infrared or laser threats to the host aircraft or other asset and other aircraft in the formation. The system can intercept, analyse and classify radiation signals targeting the host aircraft and designate priority signals for suppression through jamming the radio-electronic signals of threat systems whilst providing countermeasures action to provide an electronic barrier and interrupt incoming noise signals – Khibiny protects the host platform by shrouding it in a radio-electronic field to conceal the host platform from missile radar guidance units (Kret). The L-175B can target ground, sea surface and airborne radio electronic targets (Kret). The system also provides targeting data to the Kh-31P/PD anti-radiation missiles that are launched to destroy the target radar complex (Sukhoi & Kret). The L-175V was adopted for service on the Su-34 by a Russian Federation Presidential decree dated 18 March 2014 (KNIRTI).

Previous page: L-175V Khibiny multifunctional electronic warfare countermeasures complex carriage on the Su-34. This page: L-175B Khibiny complex on the wingtip stations of Su-34 Red 04 (top) and Red 05 (above). Sukhoi via UAC/Kret/KNIRTI

The communications complex specified for the Su-32 is the S-103 developed by JSC NPP Polet (Sukhoi). It is unclear if this equipment is standard in the Su-34 or if the more advanced S-111 system, installed in the Su-35S and Su-57 multidimensional fighter aircraft, is incorporated in late production Su-34 aircraft. The S-103 system provides for radio communications between aircraft and ground stations and telecode communications between aircraft operating in pairs or in a group (Sukhoi).

The Su-34 features a modern navigation complex with a digital multiplex channel for data exchange. The system incorporates an INS/GPS (Inertial Navigation System/Global Positioning System), receiving updates from the GLONASS (Globanaya Navigozionnaya Sputnikovaya Sistema – Global Navigation Satellite System) satellite constellation. The navigation complex provides for all-weather day and night employment of unguided bombs and rockets with a high level of accuracy when employed against radio contrast targets. The system can also be used to engage targets with guided weapons with high accuracy (Sukhoi & UAC).

Reference is often made to the Su-34 having a reconnaissance role, which would allow it to take over this role from the ageing Sukhoi Su-24MR 'Fencer 'E' tactical reconnaissance aircraft currently employed by the Russian Aerospace Forces. It is confirmed that such a capability would be pod based, but quite what the sensor suite may be incorporated is open to speculation.

In 2019, the Russian Aerospace Forces operate the Su-24MR in the tactical reconnaissance role. MODRF

In the reconnaissance role the Su-34 would be equipped with a pod mounted system as shown here in model form on the fuselage centre station. Kret

Su-34 Red 38 taxiing for take-off (top) and landing (bottom) after a demonstration flight. UAC/Rosoboronexport

Su-34 Red 38 during a demonstration flight. UAC

Sukhoi Su-34 specification – data furnished by JSC Sukhoi & UAC

Engines: development and production aircraft are powered by a pair of UEC Saturn AL-31F Series 23 afterburning turbofans, each rated at 122.59 kN (12501 kgf) with afterburner
Wing span: 14.7 m
Length: 23.34 m
Height: 6.09 m
Normal take-off weight: 38240 kg
Take-off weight with 3000 kg bomb load, 2 x R-73E, 2 x RVV-AE air to air missiles and 11400 kg fuel load: 39260 kg
Maximum internal fuel load: 11400 kg. This value, stated for the Su-32, is reduced from previous released data detailing a value of 1200 kg
Maximum flight range when configured with 6 x FAB-500 bombs, 2 x R-73E, 2 x RVV-AE and 3 x PTB-3000 (3050 litre) external fuel tanks
     H = 0 m: 1750 km
     H = Hcr, M = Mcr: 3000 km
Operational radius, low altitude flight with maximum fuel: 1130 km (Sukhoi), 1100 km (UAC) or 600 km on internal fuel – can vary depending on aircraft load out
Ferry range: 4000 km
Maximum external stores load: 8000 kg, carried on 12 stations
External fuel load: 9150 litres
Maximum speed at upper altitude: 1900 km/h without external stores
Maximum speed at sea level: 1300 km/h without external stores (conflicting Sukhoi documentation states 1400 km/h)
Maximum Mach number: 1.9
Operating ceiling, without external stores: 15000-17000 m
Take-off run at normal take-off weight: 750 m
Landing run: 1000 m when drag chute is deployed
Maximum airborne time (crew-dependent): 10 hours
In-flight refuelling system: maximum productivity (at inlet pressure of 3.5 kg/cm^2), 1100 l/m
Maximum operational overload: + 9 *g*
Armament: single GSh-301 cannon complex housed internally in the starboard wing root with 150 rounds of ammunition
Primary Sensors: Sh-141-02 electronically scanned phased-array antenna radar; Platan laser television sighting station and L-175V Khibiny electronic warfare complex
Crew: 2, pilot and navigator/weapon system operator

Top: Su-34 Red 38 during a demonstration flight armed with aerodynamic examples of the Kh-31 series supersonic air to surface missile and R-73E and R-27ER1 air to air missiles. Above: A pair of Russian Aerospace Forces Su-34 multifunctional strike fighters maneuver at low altitude. UAC/Sukhoi

Su-34 Red 15 (top) and Red 20 (bottom) of the Russian Air Force (Aerospace Forces from 1 August 2015). UAC/MODRF

Top: A Su-34 in clean configuration on a training flight over the Baltic Sea when it was approached by British RAF Typhoon multirole strike fighters operating from Estonia. Above: Su-34 operating with a Russian Western Military District Air Regiment on 12 January 2019. CC/MODRF

Top: Formation of Russian Aerospace Forces Su-34 strike fighters, including Red 08 and Red 11, observed from the cabin of a Su-34 in the formation. Above: Su-34 Red 31 of the Russian Aerospace Forces on 3 February 2019. MODRF

4

ARMAMENT OPTIONS

The design of the Su-34 weapon system was centred around the ability to deploy a large diversity of guided and unguided air to surface and air to air weapons from twelve external stores stations (hard points), as well as the incorporation of a fixed cannon armament housed internally (Sukhoi). At least one UAC document states 11 stations for the export standard Su-32 (UAC). The twelve external stores stations consist of eight wing stations, including two wingtip stations, two engine trunk stations and two centre fuselage stations. The wingtip stations would carry either R-73E air to air missiles or ECM (Electronic Counter Measures) pods. The fuselage, engine bay trunk, inner and intermediate wing stations can be used for heavy weapons carriage. Some of the weapons stations themselves would incorporate elements of the self-defence suite for deployment of active interference countermeasures (Sukhoi).

The Su-34 fixed armament consists of a single GSh-301 30 mm calibre automatic cannon housed in the starboard wing-root – this arrangement was carried over from the Su-27S/UB. The GSh-301, which weighs 50 kg (gun weight), features an independent water-evaporating system to cool the barrel during operation, shock-less 30 mm round chambering and gas powered extraction of expended shell casings. The cannon fires GSh-6-30 30 mm rounds (weight of round is 0.832 kg, of which the projectile weighs 0.39 kg) with a rate of fire of 1500-1800 rounds per minute (capacity is 150 rounds) at a muzzle velocity of 860 metres per second (KBP Tula).

The Su-34 air to air armament consists of the R-73E short-range infrared guided, R-27T1(ET1) (non-standard, but potentially available) medium range infrared guided air to air missile, R-27R1(ER1) SARH (Semi-Active Radar Homing) medium range air to air missile and the RVV-AE active radar guided medium range air to air missile. In addition, the Su-34 is specified for operation with the RVV-MD infrared guided and RVV-BD active radar guided air to air missiles, which are enhanced capability derivatives of the R-73E and RVV-AE respectively. The Su-34 can accommodate a maximum of six of any one type – R-73E, R-27, RVV-AE, RVV-BM or RVV-BD (Sukhoi), but can accommodate up to eight air to air missiles.

Top: Su-34 model with various air to air and air to surface stores masquerading as the Su-32 in the UAC stand at a trade show. Above The Su-34 is armed with a GSh-301 30 mm automatic cannon in the starboard wing root/fuselage join. UAC/Author

Entering service in the mid-1980's as the primary air to air armament of the Su-27S, the R-27 medium-range missile variants in service in 2019 are more capable updates of the R-27, of which a whole family of variants was developed, including the R-27R, NATO (North Atlantic Treaty Organisation) reporting name AA-10 'Alamo' A, with SARH and the R-27T, 'Alamo' B, with infrared guidance. Longer range variants were developed, designated R-27ER1 for the SARH variant and R-27ET1 for the infrared guided variant. These missiles, 'Alamo' C and 'Alamo' D respectively, are fitted with a boost sustain motor to extend engagement range.

Up to six R-27R1(ER1) missiles, launched from Aviation Trigger AKU-470/APU-470 launchers, can be carried by the Su-34 – four on wing stations and two on the engine bay trunk stations (Sukhoi & GosMKB Vympel). Two R-27T1(ET1) can be carried on wing stations (non-standard) in place of two of the R-27R1(ER1) missiles. The R-27ER1 has a length of 4.775 m; diameter, 0.26 m at solid rocket motor section and 0.23 m at control unit section; wing span, 0.803 m and control plane span, 0.972 m. The R-27ET1 dimensions are the same as those for the R-27ER1 with the exception of length, which, at 4.49 m, is slightly reduced. The R-27ER1 has a launch weight of 350 kg whilst the R-27ET1 launch weight, at 343 kg, is slightly less. Missile flight speed is Mach 4, the R-27ER1 having an engagement range of 60 to 62.5 km against a fighter aircraft size target and up to 100 km when employed against larger targets such as an AWACS (Airborne Warning and Control System) platform. The R-27ET1 has an engagement range of 80 km against a target in the forward hemisphere. Both variants are armed with a 39 kg expanding rod warhead (GosMKB Vympel & TMC).

The medium range R-27 was designed as a modular weapon, which included SARH (upper) and infrared guided (lower) variants. GosMKB Vympel

R-27 (Tactical Missiles Corporation)

Propulsion: two mode solid propellant rocket motor
Length: 4.775 m for R-27ER1 and 4.49 m for R-27ET1
Diameter: R-27ER1 and R-27ET1, 0.26 m at solid rocket section and 0.23 m at control unit section
Span: wing, 0.803 m and control plane, 0.972 m
Launch weight: R-27ER1, 350 kg; R-27ET1, 343 kg
Speed: Mach 4
Range: R-27ER1, 60-62.5 km against fighter aircraft sized targets and up to 100 km against larger targets; R-27ET1, 80 km in front hemisphere
Warhead: 39 kg expanding rod
Guidance: R-27ER1, SARH; R-27ET1, passive infrared

Su-34 configured with R-27ER1 missiles on the intermediate wing stations, R-73E missiles on the wingtip stations, Kh-31 series ASM (Air to Surface Missiles) on engine bay trunk stations and a Kh-59M series ASM on the fuselage centre station. UAC

Complementing the infrared guided R-27T1(ET1) is the smaller, shorter range, but highly agile, Vympel (TMC) R-73E (NATO reporting name AA-11 'Archer') infrared guided air to air missile, six of which can be carried, one on each of the intermediate, outer and wingtip stations. The R-73E was a generation ahead of its rivals when it entered service in the 1980's, comparable systems being fielded by NATO air arms only in the first decade of the twenty first century.

The R-73E short-range infrared guided air to air missile. GosMKB Vympel

The R-73 was developed with high agility as a design driver, augmented by the ability of the pilot of the host aircraft, be it an Su-27 or MiG-29 derivative, to cue the weapon to a target at up to 60° off-boresight via the HPS (Helmet Pointing System) or the twenty first century HMTDS (Helmet Mounted Target Designation System). A high level of manoeuvrability was achieved through incorporation of a number of design traits – four forward control fins, elevators attached to the rear fins, which are fixed, and deflector vanes positioned in the nozzle of the rocket engine (TMC).

The R-73E, which is carried on and launched from Aviation Trigger P-72-1D/DB2 series rail launchers, has a length of 2.9 m; diameter, 0.17 m; wing span, 0.51 m and a control plane span of 0.38 m, launch weight being 105 kg. The missile, which has a longer reach than most western equivalents, has a maximum engagement range of 30 km against a head-on target and a minimum engagement range of 0.3 km against a tail-on target manoeuvring at up to 12 g. The missile can be launched at altitudes from 0.02 km up to 20 km, the all-aspect passive infrared seeker head (the R-73EL features a laser proximity target sensor) guiding the missile to the target, which would then be destroyed by the 8 kg expanding rod warhead (TMC).

R-73E (Tactical Missiles Corporation)

Propulsion: solid propellant rocket motor
Length: 2.9 m
Diameter: 0.17 m
Span: fin span, 0.51 m and control plane span, 0.38 m
Launch weight: 105 kg
Range: 30 km maximum, head on and 0.3 km minimum, tail on against targets manoeuvring at up to 12 g
Engagement altitude: 0.02 to 20 km
Warhead: 8 kg high explosive expanding rod
Guidance: all-aspect passive infrared

RVV-AE active radar guided medium range air to air missile. GosMKB Vympel

The Vympel (TMC) RVV-AE active radar guided medium range air to air missiles, development of which commenced in the early 1980's, entered small-scale service with Russian trials units in the mid-1990's. Up to six RVV-AE can be carried by the Su-34 on the same stations as are employed for carriage of the SARH R-27ER1 (Sukhoi). As is the case with the R-27, carriage of the RVV-AE would reduce the number of stations available for air to surface stores carriage. The RVV-AE can engage a multitude of airborne target sets in all aspects against surface clutter – land and water – when subjected to dense electronic counter measures interference in all-weathers day and night. The design features electrically driven lattice control planes, which fold outward, and low-aspect wings on a central body, which contains the various sections, with the guidance complex at the front and the single-mode solid-fuel rocket motor at the rear. The missile incorporates an inertial/radio-corrected navigation system for guidance during the initial phase of the flight, switching to an active radar homing head, integrated with the multi-channel 'fire and forget' mode, during the terminal phase of the engagement. The target is destroyed by a multi-shaped charge rod type warhead detonated by a laser proximity sensor (TMC).

The RVV-AE, which is carried on and launched from AKU-170(E) launchers, has a length of 3.6 m; diameter, 0.2 m; wing span, 0.4 m; control plane span, 0.7 m, in flight position, with a launch weight of 175 kg. The missile has a minimum engagement range of 0.3 km in the rear hemisphere and a maximum engagement range of 80 km in the forward hemisphere, at speeds of Mach 4 class, against targets manoeuvring at up to 12 g. The missile can be launched at altitudes 0.02 km up to 25 km, the inertial, command and active-radar, in the terminal phase, guiding the missile to the target, which would then be destroyed by the 22.5 kg high explosive warhead activated by an active-radar fuse (TMC).

RVV-AE (Tactical Missiles Corporation)

Propulsion: solid propellant rocket motor
Length: 3.6 m
Diameter: 0.2 m
Wingspan: 0.4 m
Control plane span: 0.7 m in flight position
Launch weight: 175 kg
Range: minimum, 0.3 km in rear hemisphere and maximum, 80 km in front hemisphere
Engagement altitude: 0.02 to 25 km
Warhead: 22.5 kg high explosive
Fuse: active-radar
Guidance: inertial, command and active-radar in the terminal phase

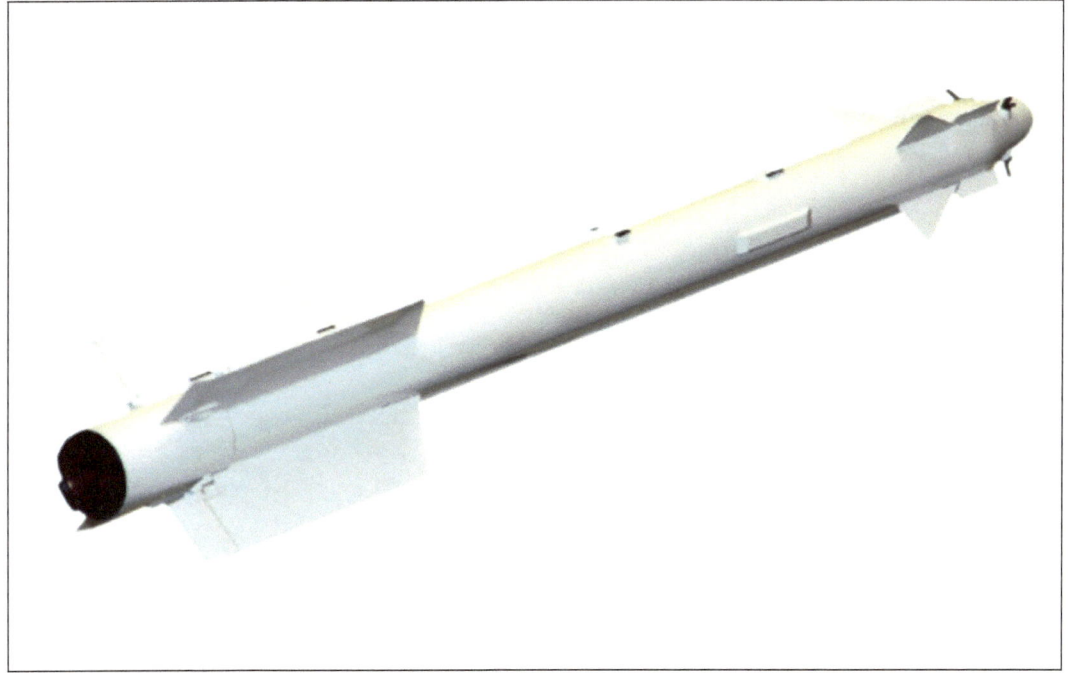

RVV-MD infrared guided short range air to air missile. GosMKB Vympel

The RVV-MD and RVV-SD, advanced variants of the R-73E and RVV-AE respectively, are armament options for the Su-34 (Sukhoi). An evolution of the R-73E, the RVV-MD is a new generation highly agile short range infrared guided missile developed to arm the new generation of Russian 4th+/4th++ and 5th generation multifunctional/multidimensional fighter aircraft. The missile is designed to engage a diversity of airborne target types operating under conditions of surface clutter and adversary counter measures (GosMKB Vympel). The RVV-MD, which is powered by a single mode engine, features enhanced anti-jamming protection over its forebear, including optical jamming, and features 'all angles passive infrared target homing (double range individual homing) with combined aero-gas dynamics control' (GosMKB Vympel). The target is destroyed by a rod-shaped warhead activated by a laser non-contact sensor in the RVV-MDL variant or a radio non-contact sensor in the RVV-MD. The RVV-MD and RVV-MDL are carried on and launched from P-72-1D/P-72-1BD2 type rail launchers (GosMKB Vympel).

The RVV-SD incorporates a number of improvements over its forebear, with longer engagement range, enhanced engagement capability, and enhanced resistance to electronic counter measures. The missile is intended for engagement of a diversity of airborne target types flying at supersonic and subsonic speeds in environmental conditions of clear and adverse weather day and night operating at all angles under conditions of surface clutter and adversary electronic counter measures (TMC).

The RVV-SD, which is carried on and launched from AKU-170(E) launchers, has a length of 3.71 m; diameter, 0.2 m; wing span, 0.42 m; rudder span, 0.68 m and a launch weight of 190 kg. The missile has a minimum engagement range of 0.3 km in the rear hemisphere and a maximum engagement range of 110 km in the forward hemisphere. The missile can be launched at altitudes of 0.02 km up to 25 km. The missile, which is powered by a single mode rocket motor, incorporates inertial command and active-radar homing in the terminal phase (GosMKB Vympel).

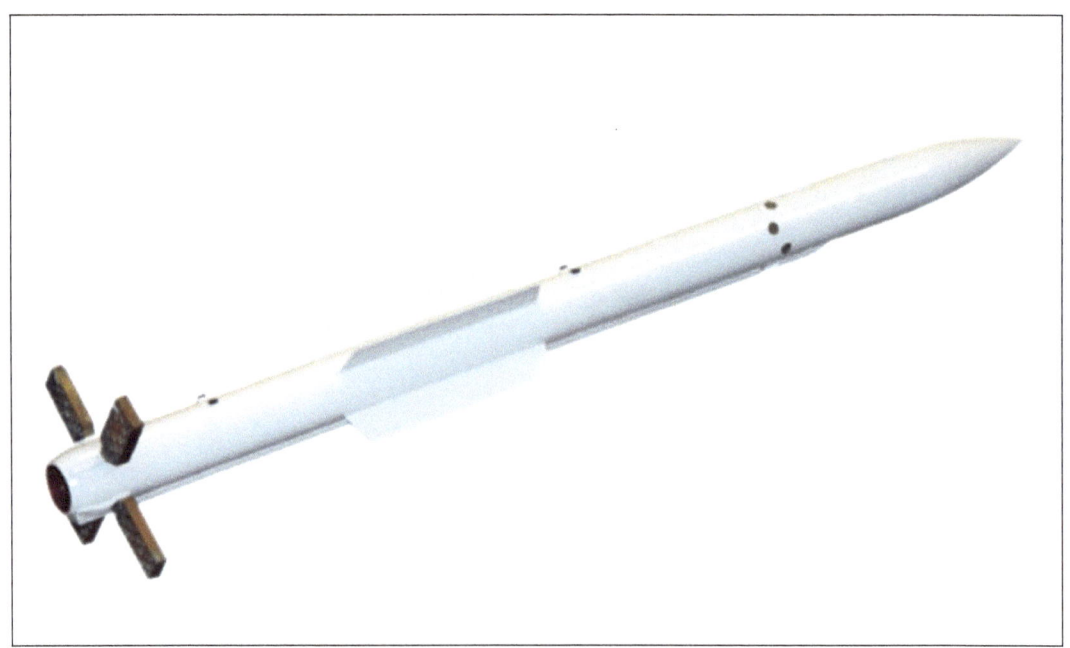

RVV-SD active radar guided medium range air to air missile. GosMKB Vympel

The Su-34 is capable of carrying a diversity of guided and unguided air to surface weapons. Available documentation confirms that the list of guided air to surface ordnance options, as of 2019, includes the following: X-31P and X-31PD air launched supersonic anti-radiation missiles, X-31A and X-31AD air launched supersonic anti-ship missiles, X-35UE air launched subsonic anti-ship missile, X-38MLE battlefield support missile, X-59MK and X-59M2E long-range air launched cruise missiles, KAB-500Kr, KAB-500OD and KAB-500S-E 500 kg class guided bomb units, KAB-1500Kr and KAB-1500LG-F-E 1500 kg class guided bomb units (Sukhoi).

The Su-34 can operate with up to six X-31A/AD (Kh-31A/AD) supersonic anti-ship missiles and X-31P/PD (Kh-31P/PD) supersonic anti-radiation missiles, all of the same variant or a mix of different variants. In the defence suppression role or the anti-ship role the six X-31P/PD anti-radiation missiles or X-31A/AD anti-ship missiles are carried on the following stations: one on each of the engine bay trunk stations, one on each of the inner wing stations and one on each of the intermediate wing stations (Sukhoi).

The X-31P passive radar homing heads (interchangeable) can operate within a range of corresponding frequency bands, allowing it to engage modern radar systems, continuous-wave and pulsed systems that would constitute elements of long and medium range air to surface missile systems. The missile can also engage other emitting radar systems not necessarily part of the air defence system. The homing head autonomously searches for and locks-on to a target, or, alternatively, the launch aircraft sensors can hand down targeting information to the missile before it is launched from the AKU-58 airborne ejection unit (TMC).

The Kh-31P, which has a launch weight of ~600 kg, is 4.7 m in length; diameter, 0.36 m and wing span is 0.914 m. The missile can be launched from altitudes of 100-15000 m at a carrier platform speed of Mach 0.65-Mach 1.25, after which it flies to targets between 15-110 km distant (depending upon launch altitude) at speeds of 1000 m/s (3600 km/h). The target is destroyed by an 87 kg high explosive fragmentation warhead (TMC).

The Kh-31PD is an evolution of the Kh-31P, maximum range being increased from 110 km to 250 km, while carrying a more powerful warhead. The Kh-31PK is a modified variant of the Kh-31P carrying a larger warhead, detonated by a proximity fuse, and retaining similar operating parameters to those of the Kh-31P (TMC). This latter weapon has not been cleared as an Su-34 armament option as of 2019.

Kh-31P (Tactical Missiles Corporation)

Length: 4.7 m
Diameter: 0.36 m
Wing span: 0.914 m
Missile Launch weight: ~600 kg
Launch altitude envelope: 100-15000 m
Launch speed envelope: Mach 0.65-Mach1.25 (600-1250 km/h)
Launch range envelope: 15-110 km
Maximum cruise speed: 1000 m/s
Warhead: 87 kg high explosive fragmentation

Kh-31PD (Tactical Missiles Corporation)

Length: 5.3 m
Diameter: 0.36 m
Wing span: 0.954 m
Missile Launch weight: 715 kg
Launch altitude envelope: 0.1-15 km
Launch speed envelope: Mach 0.65-Mach 1.5 (600-1250 km/h)
Maximum launch range (carrier flight parameters, altitude, 15 km at Mach 1.5: 180-250 km
Minimum launch range, launch altitude 0.1 km: 15 km
Guidance system: inertial plus wide waveband range passive radio homing
Target location angle when launching
    target lock being under carrier: ± 15°
    target lock at the trajectory: ± 30°
Warhead: 110 kg cluster universal

Kh-31P anti-radiation missile (top) and Kh-31PD (above). TMC

The Su-34 has been cleared for operation with the X-35E/UE and X-59MK subsonic anti-ship missiles and the X-31A/AD supersonic anti-ship missile noted above. The Kh-31A, six of which can be carried, was developed as a supersonic air launched anti-ship missile intended to engage warships operating independently or as part of a larger integrated naval group. The missile, which has the same overall dimensions, similar launch weight and identical launch parameters as the Kh-31P, can be launched from the carrier aircraft singly or in salvo in clear and adverse weather conditions, against a background of surface clutter in an active jamming environment (TMC). The on-board active-radar homing head can designate targets in pre-and-post launch modes, conduct target acquisition and selection, and determines target coordinates – elevation, azimuth and range – and generates signals, which are input to the guidance system (TMC). The missile is carried on and launched from the AKU-58A ejection unit, cruising at a speed of 1000 m/s to targets 5-70 km distant (against a Destroyer size target), dependant on launch altitude. The target is then destroyed or disabled by the 95 kg warhead (TMC).

The Kh-31AD is an evolution of the Kh-31A, featuring a 15% more powerful warhead and longer range – the latter being more than twice that of the Kh-31A (TMC).

X-31A (Tactical Missiles Corporation)

Length: 4.7 m
Body diameter: 0.36 m
Wing span: 0.914 m
Launch weight: around 610 kg
Warhead weight: 94 kg
Launch altitude envelope: 0.1-10 (15) km
Launch speed envelope: Mach 0.65-Mach 1.5 (600-1250 km/h)
Maximum cruise speed: 1000 m/s
Maximum range: 50-70 km against a Destroyer size target when launched from 10-15 km altitude

---

X-31AD (Tactical Missiles Corporation)

Length: 5.3 m
Diameter: 0.36 m
Missile Launch weight: 715 kg
Warhead: 110 kg universal
Launch altitude envelope: 0.1-15 km
Launch speed envelope: Mach 0.65-Mach 1.5 (600-1250 km/h)
Maximum launch range
    (carrier flight parameters, altitude=15 km, Mach=1.5): 120-160 km
Guidance system: inertial plus active radio homing
Active radio homing head angle of sight in vertical plane: +10°/-20°.
Active radio homing head angle of sight in horizontal plane: up to ±27°
Weather conditions for use: any conditions of sea roughness up to 4.5
Note: It is estimated that an average of two hits on a modern large size Destroyer will render the target combat ineffective if not destroyed

Previous page: Mock-up of an X-31 air to surface missile exhibited at the Paris Air Salon in 2001. This page: Graphic depicting the X-31AD supersonic extended range anti-ship missile. Author/TMC

Top: A Su-34 of the Russian Aerospace Forces armed with a maximum load of six Kh-31 series air to surface missiles. Above: A Su-34 configured with Kh-31 air to surface missiles on the engine bay trunk stations and a Kh-59 series cruise missile on the centre fuselage station. Sukhoi/GosMKB Vympel

Su-34

Page 104 top: An Su-34 manoeuvres at low altitude configured with the maximum load out of six X-31 series supersonic air to surface missiles. Page 104 bottom and page 105: Su-34 Red 38 configured with X-31 series air to surface missiles and R-73E and R-27ER1 air to air missiles. Sukhoi

Up to six X-35E (Kh-35E) ((3M-24E) anti-ship missiles can be carried by the Su-34. This weapon, which is designed to destroy surface vessels, including warships displacing up to 5,000 tonnes, can be launched from warships (Uran-E ship-borne missile system), coastal missile batteries (Bal-E mobile coastal launch system) and air platforms. The aircraft launched variant has a length of 3.85 m; diameter, 0.42 m; wing span, 1.33 m and a launch weight of 520 kg. Once launched from the host aircraft, the missile, with maximum turn angle in horizontal plane after launch of ± 90°, cruises at Mach 0.8 and descends to an altitude of some 10-15 m above the sea surface. It then descends to ~4 m above the sea surface for the terminal phase of the flight, to strike targets up to 130 km distant in sea states up to 6 in an active electronic countermeasures environment. The ARGS-35E active radar seeker has an acquisition range of around 20 km, thereafter the target is locked-on and destroyed or disabled by the 145 kg high explosive penetrator warhead (TMC).

The X-35UE (Kh-35UE), which retains the same overall external dimensions as the Kh-35E, improves on the latter in a number of areas, including an improved post-launch horizontal turn capability, and maximum engagement range, which is doubled from 130 km in the Kh-35E to 260 km in the Kh-35UE (TMC).

X-35E (Tactical Missiles Corporation)

Length: 3.85 m, aircraft launched variant
Body diameter: 0.42 m
Wing span: 1.33 m
Launch weight: 520 kg, aircraft launched variant
Warhead: 145 kg high explosive penetrator
Launch range: up to 130 km
Missile flight altitude: 10-15 m en-route to target area, dropping to about 4 m in the terminal phase of the flight
Missile cruise speed: Mach 0.8
Maximum missile turn angle in horizontal plane after launch: ±90°

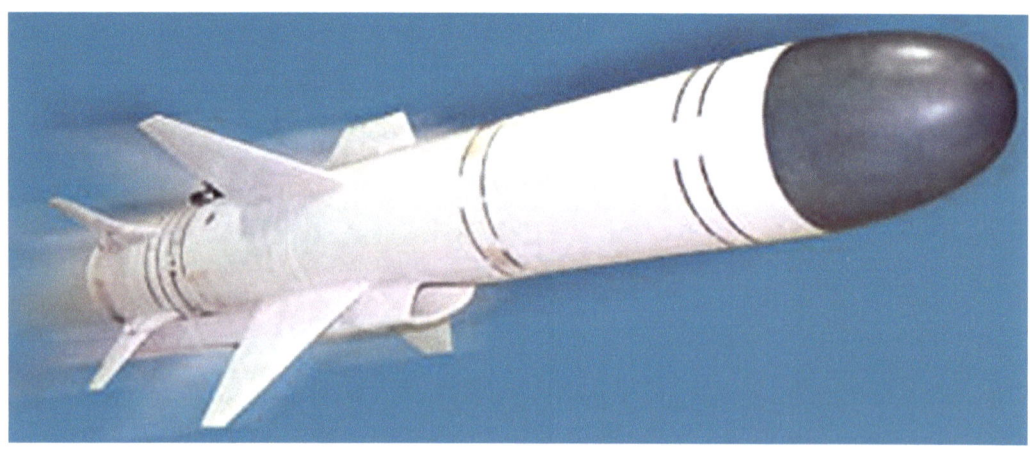

X-35E subsonic anti-ship cruise missile. TMC

X-35UE (Tactical Missiles Corporation)

Length: 3.85 m, aircraft launched variant
Body diameter: 0.42 m
Wing span: 1.33 m
Launch weight: 550 kg, aircraft launched variant
Warhead: 145 kg penetrating high explosive fragmentation
Launch range envelope: 7-260 km
Missile flight altitude over wave ridge: 10-15 m en-route to target area, dropping to ~4 m in the terminal phase of the flight
Missile cruise speed: Mach 0.8 to 0.85
Missile turn angle in horizontal plane post launch: ±130°
Guidance: inertial plus satellite navigation plus active-passive radio homing head
Maximum range of passive detection and locking with active-passive radio homing head: 50 km
Weather conditions for use: any sea conditions up to sea state 6

X-35UE extended range subsonic anti-ship cruise missile. TMC

The Su-34 can carry a maximum of three X-59M2E (Kh-59M2E) missiles of the 'Ovod-ME' complex for operations against fixed surface targets for which coordinates are known, such as buildings or bridges. The missile, which can be deployed in environmental conditions of fair weather and poor visibility day and night, has a casing length of 5.7 m; casing diameter, 0.38 m at the main body (excluding engine); wing span, 1.3 m and a launch weight of up to 960 kg. The missile can be launched from carrier aircraft flying at speeds of 600-1100 km/h (~Mach 0.4-Mach 0.9) at launch altitudes of 0.2-11 km, before flying to targets at ranges out to 115-140 km (dependant on launch parameters), cruising at Mach 0.72-0.88 at cruise altitudes of 0.007 (over sea surface) or 0.05, 01, 1.0, 2.0 or 6.1 km (over land) (TMC).

The X-59M2E is guided by an APK-9/E Ovod targeting pod carried by the launch aircraft, with a datalink to the missile. Prior to missile launch, target coordinates are downloaded for the inertial guidance phase via the datalink. The control system, consists of an 'aiming and automatic control system on the basis of inertial system unit + uncontrolled emergency jettison + low level television (imaging infrared)', colloquially referred to as a translational command aiming system (TMC). The X-59M2E missile has a stated accuracy of 2 to 3 m in manual mode and 5 to 7 m in automatic mode, the target being destroyed by the penetrating and shaped charge warheads of 320 kg and 283 kg respectively (TMC).

While the X-59M2E can be employed against land targets, the X-59MK (Kh-59MK) can be employed against sea surface targets. The X-59MK has a casing length of 5.7 m; casing diameter, 0.38 m at the main body (excluding engine) and 0.42 m at the nose section; wing span, 1.3 m and a launch weight of up to 930 kg. The missile can be launched from carrier aircraft platforms flying at speeds of 600-1100 km/h at launch altitudes of 0.2-11 km, before flying to targets at ranges out to 285 km, cruising at 900-1050 km/h at cruise altitudes of 10-15 m above the sea surface, dropping to 4-7 m in the terminal phase of the flight (TMC). The ARGS-59E active radar seeker, a derivative of the TV/command guidance unit installed in the X-59ME, provisions for the missile to home on radio-contrast surface targets in conditions up to sea state 6, thereafter the target is destroyed or disabled by the 320 kg penetrator warhead (TMC).

X-59MK (Tactical Missiles Corporation)

Length: 5.7 m
Diameter: main body minus engine, 0.38 m and 0.42 m at nose
Wing span: 1.3 m
Launch weight: not more than 930 kg
Warhead: 320 kg penetrator
Range: Maximum, 285 km against a Destroyer size target and 145 km against a boat size target. Minimum, 5.25 km
Launch envelope: can be launched by aircraft at speeds of Mach 0.5 to 0.9 (600-1000 km/h) at altitudes from 0.2 to 11 km
Missile speed: 900-1050 km/h
Missile flight altitude: 10-15 m over sea, dropping to 4-7 m in the terminal phase of the flight

X-59M2E of the Ovod missile system (top) and X-59MK cruise missile (bottom). TMC

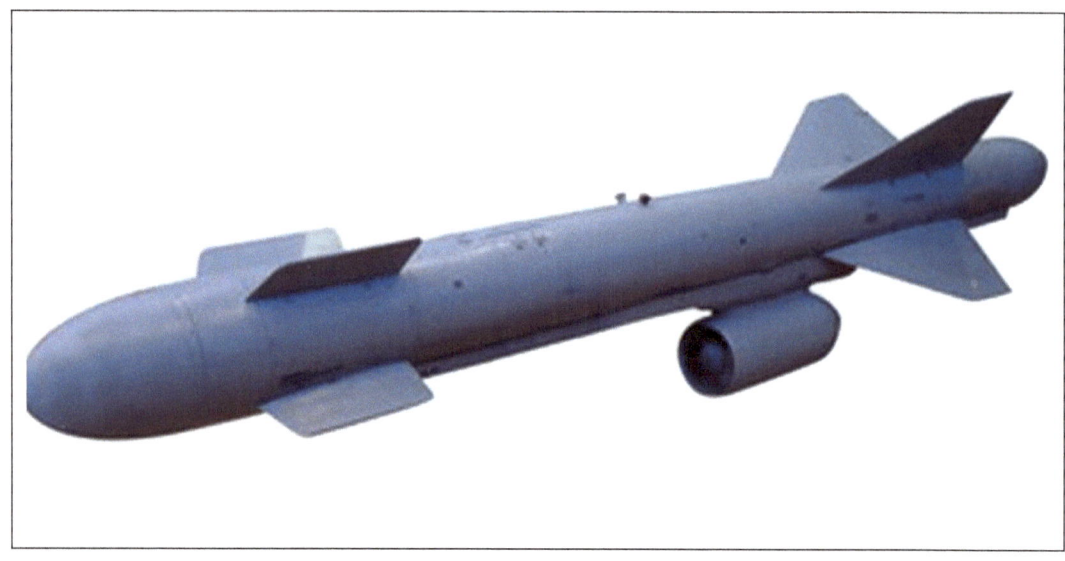

The enhanced capability variant of the X-59MK, designated X-59MK2, is not stated to be a Su-34 stores option as of 2019. TMC

For operations over the battlefield the Su-34 can be armed with X-38ME (Kh-38ME) derivative air launched battlefield missiles to destroy targets ranging from soft to reinforced/armoured. The weapon can also be employed against sea surface targets. The main difference in the variants of the missile are in payload and guidance: X-38MAE (Kh-38MAE) with inertial plus active radar guidance; X-38MKE (Kh-38MKE) with inertial plus satellite guidance; X-38MTE (Kh-38MTE) with inertial plus thermal imaging guidance and X-38MLE (Kh-38MLE) with inertial plus semi-active laser guidance. All variants are armed with a 250 kg high explosive fragmentation warhead except the X-38MKE, which is fitted with a cluster munitions warhead (TMC). As of 2019, the X-38MLE is specified for operations with the Su-32 and Su-34 – a maximum of six can be carried (Sukhoi).

X-38ME (Tactical Missiles Corporation)

Length: 4.2 m
Body diameter: 0.31 m
Wing span: 1.14 m
Maximum launch weight: 520 kg
Warhead weight: 250 kg class
Range: 3-70 km (TMC also provides a launch range of 200-12000 m)
Speed: Mach 2.2, maximum
Missile turn angle in horizontal plane after launch: ±80°
Fuse type: contact
Motor type: two-phase solid-propellant motor
Guidance: inertial plus semi-active laser (X-38MLE)

X-38ME air to surface missile. TMC

The Su-34 is cleared to operate with several variants of KAB guided bomb units: KAB-500Kr, KAB-500OD, KAB-500S-E, KAB-1500Kr and KAB-1500LG-F-E – six of each of the KAB-500 series or three of the KAB-1500 series able to be carried (Sukhoi). The KAB-500S-E is a satellite-navigation guided bomb unit for employment against fixed surface targets with an accuracy of 7-12 m CEP (Circular Error Probability) – the weapon features three delay modes on impact. Target coordinates are imputed to the bombs guidance unit prior to release from the carrier aircraft. Overall bomb weight is 560 kg, of which the warhead unit weights 460 kg, 195 kg of which is high explosive. The weapon can be released at altitudes of 0.5-5 km at carrier platform speeds of 550-1100 km/h (TMC & Rosoboronexport).

The KAB-500Kr is a concrete piercing guided bomb unit with electro-optical correlation TV guidance for employment against surface targets, with an accuracy up to 4-7 m CEP. The coordinates of the target are imputed to the bombs guidance unit prior to release from the carrier aircraft. Overall bomb weight is 520 kg, of which the concrete piercing (high explosive penetrator) warhead unit weights 380 kg, 100 kg of which is high explosive. The weapon can be released from the carrier platform at altitudes of 0.5-5 km at carrier platform speeds of 550-1100 km/h (TMC & Rosoboronexport).

The KAB-1500Kr is a concrete piercing guided bomb unit with electro-optical correlation TV guidance for employment against hardened surface targets, with an accuracy of 4-7 m CEP. The coordinates of the target are imputed to the bombs guidance unit prior to release from the carrier aircraft. Overall bomb weight is 1525 kg, of which the concrete piercing (high explosive penetrator) warhead unit (with three fuse delay modes) is 1100 kg, 210 kg of which is high explosive. The weapon can be released at altitudes of 1-8 km at carrier platform speeds of 550-1100 km/h. The KAB-1500LG-F-E is a laser gyro-stabilised seeker head guided bomb unit for engagement of fixed ground targets (TMC & Rosoboronexport).

	KAB-500Kr	KAB-500-OD	KAB-1500Kr
Launch weight:	520 kg	370 kg	1525 kg
Warhead weight:	380 kg	250 kg	1170 kg
High explosive:	100 kg	250 kg	440 kg
Length:	3.05 m	3.05 m	4.63 m
Diameter:	0.35 m	0.35 m	0.58 m
Empennage:	0.75 m	0.75 m	0.85 m (folded)
Release altitude:	0.5-5 km	0.5-5 km	1-8 km
Carrier speed:	---------------------------- 550-1100 km/h ----------------------------		
Root mean Square deviation:	4-7 m	4-7 m	4-7 m
Warhead type:	concrete piercing (high explosive penetrator)	high explosive fuel air	high explosive

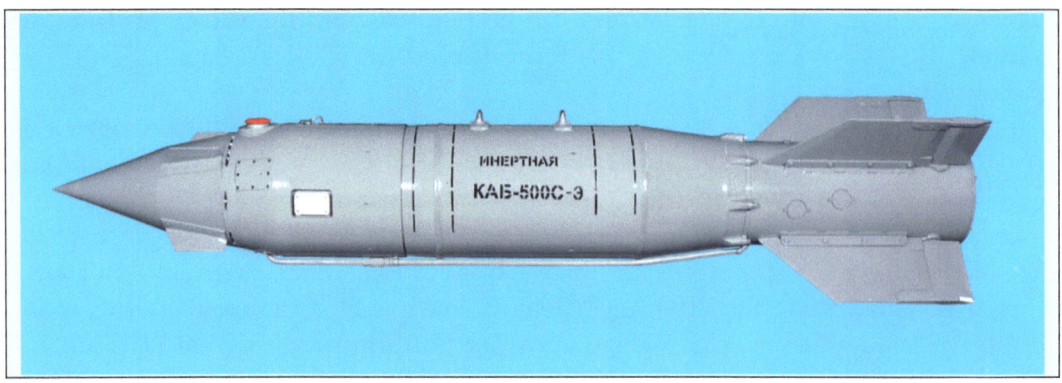

Su-34

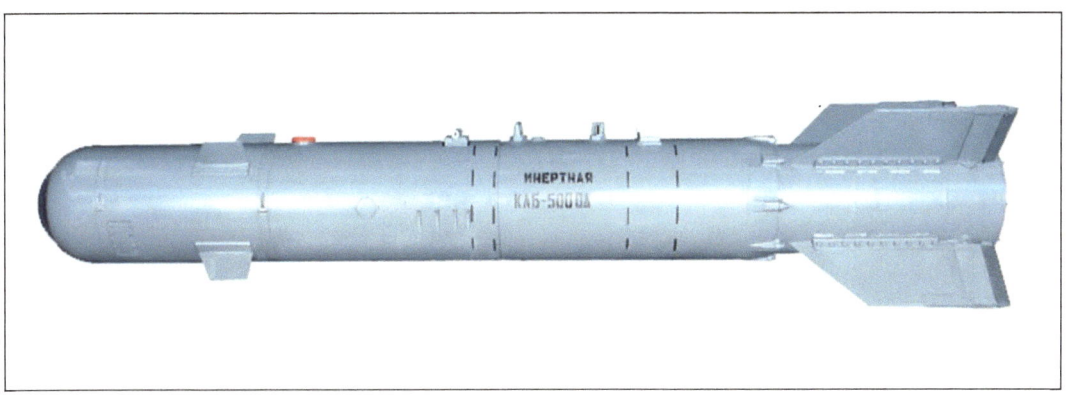

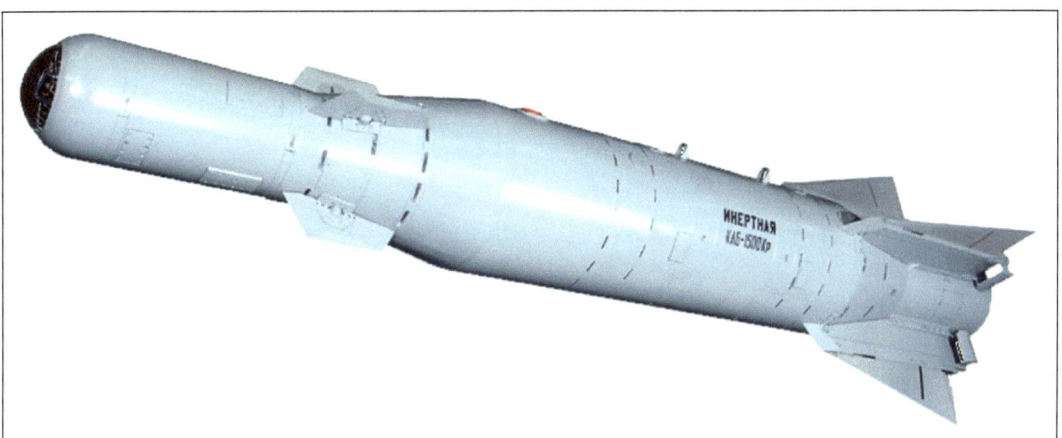

Page 112 top: The KAB-1500LG-F-E guided bomb unit, which has a diameter of 0.58 m and a wingspan of 0.85 m with control surfaces retracted and 1.3 m with control surfaces extended, has a launch weight of 1525 kg, warhead weight, 1120 kg, of which 440 kg is high explosive, with three delay modes for the contact fuse. The weapon can be launched at altitudes of 1-8 km at carrier platform speeds of 550-1100 km/h. Accuracy is 4-7 m CEP. Page 112 bottom: KAB-500S-E 500 kg class guided bomb unit. Page 113: KAB-500OD 500 kg class guided bomb unit (top), KAB-1500LG-F-E 1500 kg class guided bomb unit (centre) and KAB-1500Kr guided bomb unit (bottom). Rosoboronexport/ GNPP Region

KAB-500S-E 500 kg class reinforced concrete piercing guided bomb units being loaded on to the engine bay stations of an Su-34 of the Russian Aerospace Group operating in the Syrian Arab Republic in support of the Syrian Arab Army fighting ISIL and other opposition groups during the Syrian civil war, circa late 2015. MODRF

When carrying small calibre unguided bombs the Su-34 would be equipped with an MBD3-U6-68 type multi-lock girder holder (multiple ejector stores station) (GosMKB Vympel). The station incorporates six DZ-57DA stores locks, which can accommodate bombs of 50, 100 or 250 kg weight class. The BD4-USKB and BD4-USKM-B stores stations are incorporated for the carriage and release of stores with weights up to 1500 kg class. These stations can also accommodate the PTB-3000 external fuel tank.

Bomb load outs can include a maximum of 32 x OFAB-100-120 general purpose bombs and up to 28 x FAB-250 (OFAB-250-270), general purpose bombs. The 500 kg class unguided bombs available can include FAB-500, RBK-500 or BETAB-500, up to eight of which can be carried – one of each of the inner and intermediate wing stations, two on fuselage centre stations and one on each of the engine bay stations (MODRF).

The FAB-500 M-62 is a general purpose high explosive weapon designed to destroy a diversity of target types – buildings, soft skinned vehicles and field fortifications. The FAB-500 M-62 has a length of 2470 mm; diameter, 400 mm and weighs 500 kg (high explosive warhead weight is 300 kg) and can be deployed at altitudes from 570-12000 m at carrier platform speeds of 500-1900 km/h (Rosoboronexport).

The FAB-500 M-62 is the standard 500 kg class unguided general purpose high explosive weapon cleared for carriage by the Su-34. Rosoboronexport

Top: FAB-500 M-62 500 kg class general purpose bomb being loaded on to a Su-34 of the Russian Aerospace Group operating against ISIL targets in Syria, circa 2015. Above: BETAB-500 500 kg class reinforced concrete piercing bomb on a Su-24M. MODRF/Rosoboronexport

The BETAB-500 is a 500 kg class weapon designed to penetrate reinforced concrete and other hardened structures. The weapon can penetrate reinforced concrete up to 1 m in thick after travelling through 3 m of soil. Basic characteristics include a length of 2200 mm; diameter, 350 mm and weight, 477 kg (warhead high explosive weight is 98 kg). The weapon can be released at altitudes of 30-5000 m at carrier platform speeds up to 1200 km/h (Rosoboronexport).

Page 117 top: Su-34 development aircraft (T-10V-7), White 47, dropping multiple unguided bombs during a weapon clearance phase of development trials. **Page 117 bottom:** An Su-34 takes off to deliver a bomb strike – FAB-500 M-62 500 kg class general purpose bombs – on range targets in Voronezh region, Russia, circa February/March 2019. **Page 118:** An Su-34 takes-off to bomb range targets in Russia – FAB-500 M-62 500 kg class general purpose bombs – on 16 February 2019. UAC/MODRF

Unguided rocket armament options include a maximum of 80 x 80 mm S-80KOM/Ts-8BM carried in B8M1 rocket pods, each of which contain twenty rockets, which can be launched singly or in salvo fire under environmental conditions of ambient temperatures ±60° Centigrade. The B8M1 rocket pod, which can be carried on the inner and intermediate wing stations, can be substituted by the B13L pod containing 5 x 122 mm S-13T unguided rockets, a maximum of 20 of which could be carried, five in each of four pods. Like the B8M1 pod, the B13L can launch its rockets singly or in salvo under the same environmental operating conditions. The B8M1 and B13L pods are carried on BD3-USK-B beam holders (GosMKB Vympel). An alternative armament option is the 266 mm S-25, S-250OFM-PU, four of which can be carried on the same stations as the B8M1 and B13L rocket pods. Sukhoi documentation shows that up to eight of the P-50T weapons can be carried (Sukhoi).

Other external stores include external fuel tanks of the PTB-3000 (3050 litre) type and electronic warfare complexes that would be carried on the wingtip stations, discussed in the previous chapter.

Top: A Su-34 (T-10V development aircraft) launches unguided rockets during a weapon integration phase of the overall Su-34 development program. Above: A T-10V development aircraft configured with four rocket pods on the inner and intermediate wing stations and unguided bombs on the engine bay stations and fuselage centre stations. Sukhoi

Top: Model of the Su-34, configured with long-range cruise missiles, at the 1997 Paris Air Salon. Above: Graphic rendering of a Su-34, in Russian Naval Aviation markings, launching a long-range cruise missile. Author/NAPO (NAZ)

5

SU-34 – RUSSIAN AEROSPACE GROUP, SYRIA OPERATIONS

The Russian Aerospace Group, which had, over the previous few weeks, formed at Hmeymim air base, located in the northern Latakia province of Syria, formally commenced combat operations on 30 September 2015. These operations would be conducted over Syria in response to a request to the Russian Federation from the government of the Syrian Arab Republic for assistance in its fight against ISIL (Islamic State of Iraq and the Levant) and other groups deemed to be terrorist organisations embroiled in the Syrian civil war. By summer 2015, civil war had raged within the Syrian Arab Republic for over four years, ever more external participants being drawn in as various groups and nations began picking at the bones of a nation in turmoil.

It would certainly not be an understatement to say that, going into summer 2015, the situation was bleak for the regime of Syrian President, Bashar al Assad, which was fighting on several fronts against many enemies. In addition, the Syrian regime faced a growing threat from western powers sensing an opportunity to replace that regime with a western backed government, despite the failures of such policies in Iraq, Afghanistan and Libya – all three countries being in the throes of turmoil following Anglo-US and other NATO (North Atlantic Treaty Organisation) nation campaigns and invasions. These enterprises had resulted in abject failure in that all three examples left those countries in lawless states of civil war. Particularly in the cases of Iraq and Libya, the western campaigns would lead to the rise of extremist organizations like ISIL, which garnered much support from a populace that had been subjected to tyranny from their own governments and, in the case of Iraq, more than two decades of bombing, economic sanctions, invasion and occupation by the major western powers.

The rise of ISIL had beckoned black tidings for Syria as it advanced across that nation's borders from Iraq, taking ground previously sparsely defended by government forces, the bulk of which was tied down fighting against western backed opposition groups. As ISIL took over more ground the western coalition (including their Middle East allies such as Saudi Arabia) provided increased support –

financially, with armament supplies and military assistance (mainly with armed air support provided to those groups termed the 'moderate opposition', a label applied as dressing to make backing such groups palatable to American and European populations, despite the indelible fact that they were operating alongside, and often integrated with, extremist organisations like Nusra Front, fighting Syrian government forces). Western military support was provided mainly against ISIL. No direct military support was openly provided against Syrian government forces, although a number of air/missile strikes would be launched against Syrian government forces under various pretext and others, termed as accidents or mistakes.

By late summer 2015, Syrian government forces had yielded large areas of Syria's land mass to western backed opposition groups and ISIL, which appeared all conquering. The so called moderate opposition, with support from the western coalition and other partner nations, took advantage of the Syrian government forces fight against ISIL to try and take ground, or consolidate ground already held, but also lost ground to ISIL at the same time. As noted above, often the line between ISIL, other extremists and western backed opposition groups was blurred as they integrated in their fight against the Syrian regime that was supported militarily by Russia and Iran.

The Russian air campaign in the Syrian Arab Republic could be simplified into four main categories: tactical support to Syrian government ground forces conducting field operations against ISIL and other opposition groups; infrastructure and supply route interdiction against ISIL and other opposition group occupied areas; oil infrastructure and transportation interdiction and air defence, the latter taking an increasingly visible role following the ultimately unsuccessful unorthodox NATO attempts to interfere with the Russian operation in late November 2015 – this had the effect of forcing operational changes in that Su-34 aircraft had begun operating with R-27ER1 medium range semi-active radar guided air to air missiles to counter the threat from NATO warplanes. The various air defence enhancements, which included the installation of S-400 long range and Pantsir S-1 short range surface to air missile systems, protected Russian bases and air operations, which were not challenged further by NATO. There were, of course, other areas of operations, not least of which was logistics resupply, air base defence and search and rescue.

The Russian air campaign was conducted within the Syrian command structure, a joint Russian/Syrian command centre being located at Hmeymim air base to this end. The Russia campaign was initiated under the auspices of the Aerospace Group based at Hmeymim air base, although it would also call on other sea, land and air based assets, the latter based on Russian territory. Initially the Aerospace Group consisted of Sukhoi Su-24M strike aircraft, Su-34 multifunctional strike fighter aircraft, Su-25SM ground attack aircraft, Su-30SM multidimensional strike fighter aircraft, a number of helicopters used for air base defence and search and rescue operations and UAV (Uninhabited Air Vehicles) for reconnaissance/surveillance. As the campaign progressed more Russian air assets would be committed to the operation, including carrier based aircraft, additional multirole air assets, Beriev A-50U AWACS (Airborne Warning and Control) aircraft, electronic warfare aircraft and combat helicopters of the Ka-52/K and Mi-28 types.

On the morning of 30 September 2015, Russian General, Kuralenko, in person, notified the US (United States) Military attaché in Iraq, Colonel Petro, that Russia would commence strike missions over Syria later that day. From the last four months of 2015 through 2017, the Russian air campaign in support of the Syrian Arab Army broke the back of ISIL and other opposition groups leading to the liberation of large swathes of land, towns and cities. As ISIL drew much of its forces away from North Eastern Syria to reinforce the areas under military pressure from the Syrian government forces, the western backed SDF (Syrian Democratic Forces) dominated by Kurdish forces (this included a large number of foreigners, effectively constituting a poorly trained invasion force) began to make headway to fill the vacuum. ISIL forces were transferred from Iraq to join the fight against Syrian government forces in the eastern enclave of Deir-ez-Zor, which was besieged by ISIL. The Syrian army offensives would open up the road to central Syria supporting Syrian Army operations to liberate the historical cultural site of Palmyra, which was liberated in March 2016, and, after ISIL recaptured the city, it was liberated for the second time in 2017. Palmyra had a strategic significance as a hub to many of the major conflict zones in Syria, including the bastion of Deir-ez-Zor in the East of Syria. By early August 2017, ISIL was in steep decline all across Syria as a result of the pressure being applied by the Syrian Army backed by Russian air power. This pressure had the effect of continuing to draw ISIL forces away from North and northeastern areas of Syria, allowing the western backed SDF, backed by small contingents of American and European nation ground forces to occupy those lands. The Syrian/Russian operations would be the catalyst for launching new offensives that would result in ISIL, as a coordinated fighting force, being destroyed and driven from much of Syria. As the Syrian Army advanced on Deir-ez-Zor ISIL forces continued to redeploy from northern regions to counter this threat. This would lead to the fall of Raqqa (Raqqa) to the SDF forces, backed by western coalition air power, and the occupation of large swaths of land, all but abandoned by ISIL. While the Raqqa sideshow was ongoing in the North of the country, Syrian Army units encircled and destroyed large formations of ISIL forces on the road to Deir-ez-Zor. ISIL forces were severely degraded by the Syrian Army and Russian air power allowing the main ground force to advance on El Qder. The destruction of ISIL as an organized fighting body in these areas allowed the Syrian army to rapidly advance at 30-40 km per day in the race to Deir-ez-Zor (this was a race with SDF forces filling the void left with the large scale withdrawals of ISIL forces to meet the Syrian army offensive), liberating the large towns of El-Khom, Br-Kdem and capturing the Memnis oil field, before encircling ISIL forces in the area of Te-Teiba. Around the same time, Syrian Army units liberated Sukhne to the east of Palmyra (MODRF).

Following the ejection of extremist forces from Aleppo, the second liberation of Palmyra from ISIL control and the breaking of the siege of Deir-ez-Zor in the East, Russia's campaign was officially ended toward the end of 2017 in regards to a large-scale anti-ISIL operation. Significant air assets were retained in Syria to provide small scale air support for Syrian Army ground operations and counterstrike operations against extremist/opposition forces being driven out of most of the remaining pockets of resistance west of the Euphrates River – the operations, centred on containing extremist forces in their last major bastion of Idlib, continuing in 2019.

The following is a chronological list of significant dates and events in the Russian Air campaign in regards to Su-34 operations:

30 September 2015: On the first day of combat operations, 30 September 2015, eight separate target areas were struck by Su-24M, Su-34 and Su-25SM ground attack aircraft. Targets in the main consisted of ammunition storage, POL (Petroleum Oil Lubricants) storage, combat vehicles and command and communications posts (MODRF).

1 October 2015: Su-34 strike aircraft attacked a target described as an ISIL training base close to Madan-Jadid and a headquarters facility in the area of Cassert-Farahj, located to the south west of Raqqa. Post-strike assessment indicated that the target was rendered 'inoperative' and that the training facility was 'completely destroyed' (MODRF).

3 October 2015: An MODRF briefing document stated that Su-24M and Su-34 strike aircraft had flown 20 sorties, presumably the previous day, although it was indicated that at least some of these sorties may have been flown on the evening of 2 October and or the night of 2/3 October. Su-34's struck a 'hardened command centre' and an 'underground bunker' near Raqqa with BETAB-500 reinforced concrete penetrating bombs. Another Su-34 strike targeted what was described as an ISIL facility near to Maarat al-Nuuman, Idlib, with KAB-500Kr guided bomb units, apparently hitting a number of facilities, including ammunition storage, defensive fortifications, seven vehicles and POL depots. A third Su-34 strike targeted a hardened facility near Raqqa, stated to have been an ISIL command centre. This target was struck by BETAB-500 reinforced concrete penetrating bombs, which resulted in huge explosions emanating from the bunker (MODRF).

4 October 2015: Over the course of the previous 24 hours, 20 strike sorties were flown against ten targets by Su-24M, Su-25SM and Su-34's. Four targets, described as command posts, were destroyed by BETAB-500 concrete penetrating bombs (MODRF), these apparently attributable to Su-34 strikes. A target, described as a 'special training camp' and an ammunition storage facility in the area of Al-Tabqa, Raqqa province, was struck by KAB-500 series guided bombs dropped from Su-34 strike aircraft, both targets being assessed as destroyed by post-strike OM (Objective monitoring (damage assessment)) (MODRF).

5 October 2015: The MODRF reported that over the course of the previous 24 hours – apparently sorties flown between late afternoon/evening of 4 October into the early morning of 5 October – Su-24M, Su-25SM and Su-34 aircraft bombed nine targets. Su-24M and Su-34 aircraft struck three targets at Talbiseh, Homs, two of these being described as ammunition storage depots. Daytime operations on 5 October included 14 sorties by Su-24M, Su-25SM and Su-34 aircraft, during the course of which ten target areas were struck (MODRF).

6 October 2015: Su-34 aircraft were operating in the airspace near Gnam, Latakia, Province, where they bombed an ISIL fortified position which was claimed by the MODRF as being destroyed, along with munitions and POL storages (MODRF).

8 October 2015: A MODRF briefing stated that 22 sorties had been flown by Su-24M, Su-25SM and Su-34 aircraft that night, 27 separate targets being struck. It is

unclear if those sorties were flown earlier on the 8th or perhaps the reference was intended for the previous night of the 7-8 October. During the course of these operations a force of Su-24M and Su-34 aircraft struck eight targets in the province of Homs. Post-strike OM indicated that fortified positions were destroyed with a number of secondary explosions being observed, these apparently being the result of exploding munition and fuel storages. A Su-34 employed BETAB-500 concrete penetrating bombs against a fire position with underground bunkers in the vicinity of al-Safsafah. Su-25SM and Su-34 aircraft conducted a combined 11 strikes on ISIL targets in Hamah and Raqqa provinces (MODRF).

9 October 2015: Sometime during the course of the afternoon/evening or night of 8 October and the morning of 9 October, a headquarters/command centre of the Liwa al-Haqq grouping in Raqqa Province was destroyed by one or more KAB-500Kr guided bombs launched from an Su-34 (MODRF).

12 October 2015: A MODRF briefing document stated that over the previous 24 hours data, which had been obtained by reconnaissance assets, had located a facility that it was determined was used for training foreign personnel joining extremist groups in Syria. The target was subsequently attacked by Su-34 aircraft, much damage being inflicted (MODRF).

14 October 2015: An MODRF briefing held on this date stated that over the course of the previous 24 hours an air strike, about 21 km south of Aleppo, destroyed a facility that was apparently used to repair armoured vehicles and convert off-road vehicles to carry weapons, such as mortar (artillery), large calibre machine guns and ZU-23 23 mm anti-aircraft guns. The type of aircraft that conducted this strike was not stated in the briefing document, but it was most likely to have been either Su-24M or Su-34. A Su-34 destroyed an ISIL command centre near Aleppo with a precision guided weapon (MODRF), a KAB-500 derivative bomb. To the south of Aleppo a Su-34 destroyed a facility that was stated by the MODRF to be used as an ISIL sapper training facility (MODRF).

The main aviation strike assets of the Russian Aerospace Group based at Hmeymim air base was the Sukhoi Su-34 multifunctional strike fighter (page 125 top), the Sukhoi Su-24M2 variable-geometry (swing-wing) strike aircraft (page 125 bottom) and the Sukhoi Su-25SM ground attack aircraft (page 126). All three aircraft types are here operating from Hmeymim air base with unguided munitions. MODRF

15 October 2015: An Su-34 destroyed a fortified position in the Eastern Ghouta region of Damascus Province that contained a captured Osa SAM (Surface to Air Missile) system. The concrete fortified bunker system was destroyed by a KAB-500S-E reinforced concrete penetrating guided bomb unit, resulting in the destruction of

the missile system. An air reconnaissance in the area of Khan Shaykhun in Mama Province provided data on a fortified position that included an ISIL artillery battery. Once the data was checked a mixed force of Su-34 strike aircraft and Su-25SM ground attack aircraft was launched in an operation that resulted in the destruction of 'six artillery guns and four off road vehicles equipped with mortars' (MODRF).

18 October 2015: An MODRF briefing held on this date stated that over the course of the previous 24 hours Su-34 strike aircraft struck an underground fortification, which apparently included a vast network of tunnels, in support of operations of the Syria army (MODRF).

19 October 2015: An MODRF briefing held on this date stated that over the course of the previous 24 hours strike missions included an attack on an underground complex claimed to feature a network of tunnels that emerged into inhabited areas of Jubb al-Zarus in Hama Province. This target was destroyed by an undisclosed number of KAB-500S-E guided bomb units launched from an Su-34 (MODRF).

20 October 2015: An Su-34 bombed what the MODRF described as 'a mini-plant manufacturing explosive devices and unguided rocket', in the area of Hatla in Deir-ez-Zor Province, the target being destroyed (MODRF). Other Su-34 operations over Deir-ez-Zor included an attack on what the MODRF described as command and communication centers that were being utilised to coordinate ground forces in the area facing besieged Syrian Army units. The target, which was apparently located in a former post office, was destroyed by a KAB-500 series guided bomb unit. On the night of 20 October an Su-34 bombed a command and control target. The attack was the culmination of an operation quickly put together following interceptions of radio traffic that indicated a meeting was planned for the commanders of opposition groups (undisclosed groups) that were then operating in the area of Sarmin, Idlib Province. Further intelligence gathering provided the timing and location of the planned meeting, which was then put under constant surveillance. On the night of 20 October, a grouping of nine off-road vehicles, armed with large calibre machine guns, was observed at the location. The Su-34, which had been launched with the specific task of bombing the location, released at least one KAB-500 series guided bomb unit, completely destroying the target. Radio interceptions known to have been gathered around this time included certain conversations signaling the commencement of negotiations between ISIL and the Jabhat an-Nusra group for the coordination of attacks against Syrian government forces and government controlled areas (MODRF). However, it is unclear if this subject was the area of electronic intelligence concerning the 20 October attack on the command and control target.

22 October 2015: At this stage in the Russian campaign the MODRF acknowledged a change in tactics in that early in the campaign strike/attack aircraft mainly operated in pairs, but now two or more targets were routinely allocated to a single aircraft. This tactic change facilitated a reduction in overall sortie numbers allocated to strike missions. It was becoming clear at this stage of the campaign that the attacks by Su-34 strike aircraft were typically conducted from altitudes in the region of 5000 m, somewhat lower than the 6000 m altitude that the majority of Su-24M2 attacks were being conducted from. It was clarified that the main focus of the Russian operations concerned providing battlefield support for Syrian Army units engaged in operations

to retake towns and villages that had been occupied by ISIL and Jabhat an-Nusra forces, as well as other opposition groups, and that intelligence data confirmed that ISIL losses in Syria, primarily to Russian air attacks, had led to the transfer of ISIL forces from Iraq (MODRF).

26 October 2015: Operations over the previous three days included an attack by a Su-34 on an ISIL command centre located by UAV reconnaissance near Zaytan, Aleppo province. This facility, which was destroyed by a direct hit of an undisclosed bomb type, was apparently used to coordinate the operations of opposition forces facing Syrian Army units in the area of Kwaires air base (MODRF).

Page 128: Su-34 Red 25 landing at Hmeymim air base following a bombing mission (top) and Su-34 Red 03 at Hmeymim with KAB-500S-E guided bomb units on the engine bay stations, unguided bombs on the inner wing stations and R-73E air to air missiles on the intermediate wing stations (bottom). **Page 129:** Su-34 Red 25 landing at Hmeymim following a bombing mission, with some of its ordnance remaining (top) and Su-34's at dispersal at Hmeymim (bottom). MODRF

2 November 2015: Missions conducted over the previous two days included the bombing of a munitions depot and training camp in the suburbs of Aleppo that was used to train foreigners joining extremist opposition forces. This target, which was discovered through reconnaissance of the area and intelligence on the ground, was destroyed by several direct hits of undisclosed bomb type launched by at least one Su-34. Another Su-34 strike in Aleppo Province destroyed a facility that was stated by the MODRF to manufacture explosive devices (MODRF).

3 November 2015: An Su-34 bombed an ISIL target near Tadmor in Deir-ez-Zor Province and another bombed a target at Itria to the East of Aleppo, both targets apparently being struck by KAB-500 series guided bomb units. The coordinates of the second target was supplied by elements of the opposition forces that were involved in in-fighting with ISIL over dominance of the area (MODRF).

5 November 2015: Su-34 strike aircraft were active in the area of Raqqa Province where two fortified positions, located on the approaches to the city of Raqqa, were attacked. Several direct bomb hits destroyed the fortifications as well as four vehicles, a mix of unarmoured and armoured. A facility, referred to as a Jabhat al-Nusra terrorist training camp, which had been located near Al-Muhasan in Deir-ez-Zor Province, was attacked by a Su-34, which released KAB-500 series guided bomb units. This resulted in the destruction of much of the facilities infrastructure, which included a munitions depot (MODRF).

9 November 2015: In the suburbs of the town of al Zebra, Idlib Province, a command centre, stated to be the used for coordination of Jabhat al-Nusra group operations in the Idlib-Aleppo Provinces, was attacked by a Su-34. Post-strike assessment showed that the facility had been destroyed by the single KAB-500 series guided bomb released from the Su-34. Su-34 operations in Raqqa destroyed two munitions depots located in the suburbs of the city (MODRF).

It was noted that ISIL had, by this, time changed tactics to adapt to the new threat that was introduced with the commencement of Russian air strikes on 30 September 2015. Whereas previously ISIL, with a higher level of confidence, were able to withstand the low level of air strikes of the Syria air force, their forces now had to adapt to a higher level of maneuver operations and concealment to provide some protection against the Russian air strikes, which had severely adversely impacted on the groups fighting formations over the past month or so. Much of its resupply and reinforcement routes were only active at night in an attempt to afford a small measure of protection from the darkness (MODRF.

11 November 2015: During the course of the previous two days, bombing missions included a Su-34 strike launched against a Jabhat al-Nusra group underground munitions depot in the suburbs of Mahin, Homs Province. Coordinates for this target were supplied by rival opposition groups and then verified through intelligence channels. The target was struck by a BETAB-500 concrete-penetrating bomb, which resulted in the detonation of stored munitions, destroying the facility (MODRF).

13 November 2015: Missions flown over the previous two days included a Su-34 strike on an underground munitions depot in the suburbs of Jasmin, Daraa Province. The target was destroyed by a direct hit by a BETAB-500 concrete-penetrating bomb, which detonated the munitions. An Su-34 strike was launched against a Jabhat

al-Nusra group munitions depot located in the suburbs of al-Latama, Hama Province. Post-strike assessment showed that two integral buildings were destroyed along with the stored munitions (MODRF).

Page 131-132: Su-34 strike fighters of the Russian Aerospace Group operating from Hmeymim air base in the Syrian Arab Republic. MODRF

Russian aircraft continued to fly oil interdiction reconnaissance and strike sorties. During one such reconnaissance sortie a convoy of oil trucks was observed in the area of Mayadin, Deir-ez-Zor Province, moving in the direction of the Syria/Iraq border. Intelligence information indicated that the oil tankers were carrying crude oil extracted from the oil fields controlled by ISIL to a destination across the border to an ISIL controlled area of northern Iraq. An Su-34 was directed to the area and bombed the column. Post-strike assessment confirmed that all of the oil tanker trucks had been destroyed (MODRF).

17 November 2015: Over the course of two days the Russian Aerospace Group, in concert with offensive assets based in the Russian Federation – Tupolev Tu-22M3 intermediate range bombers and Tu-95MS and Tu-160 strategic missile carriers – conducted a major offensive against targets in Syria. As well as Su-34 sorties flown from Hmeymim air base, eight Su-34 sorties were flown from Southern Russia and landed at Hmeymim (MODRF).

~17 November 2015: Su-34 aircraft commenced bombing attacks on ISIL controlled oil facilities in Syria. As well as fixed facilities, the oil interdiction campaign included further attacks on road convoys. On 22 or 23 November, reconnaissance had detected two separate columns of vehicles transporting oil from ISIL controlled oil production facilities in Raqqa Province. Su-34 strike aircraft attacked the columns, destroying about 80 vehicles. In addition, an oil terminal, located 15 km to the south-west of Raqqa, was destroyed. Further south, some 50 km from Raqqa, Su-34 strike aircraft bombed an ISIL controlled oil production plant. An Su-34 bombed a column of tanker trucks on 24 November. In the east of Syria, some 50 km to the north of Deir-ez-Zor, Su-34 strike aircraft struck petroleum tanks, completely destroying the target (MODRF).

Mission types flown in the oil interdiction campaign, which continued through December 2015, included the 'free search', in which aircraft would patrol an area searching for oil tanker road traffic. Among the targets struck by Su-34's included road convoys to and from Deir-ez-Zor, 94 oil tanker/transport trucks being destroyed in strikes around 16 December (MODRF). On or around 16 December 2015, an Su-34 (this may have been part of a two-ship formation) flying a free search mission in the vicinity of Rashidya-Ghaubia, Hasakah Province, located an oil convoy, numbering 15 trucks, heading north. The Su-34 strike resulted in the apparent destruction of the convoy. There were six incidences of air attacks on oil transportation vehicles in Deir-ez-Zor and Aleppo Provinces around 28-30 December (MODRF). Although the type of aircraft employed was undisclosed, this was most likely Su-24M or Su-34.

28 December 2015: Other target sets continued to be attacked. On or around 28 December a concrete reinforced shelter that was part of a captured Osa SAM complex (location undisclosed) was destroyed by direct hit(s) from one or more BETAB-500 reinforced concrete penetrating bombs launched from an Su-34. Another Su-34 strike, on or around 28 December, materialised through information passed to the Russian command centre by an opposition group in northeast Syria. This information indicated that ISIL field commanders planned to meet at a location in the suburbs of Raqqa on 27 or 28 December. The location was placed under 24 hours a day observation by intelligence gathering assets, including UAV and satellite surveillance, which provided confirmation of the arrival of the ISIL leaders at the designated location. An Su-34 was directed to the area and destroyed the target building with one or more KAB-500 series guided bomb units (MODRF).

Top: The drogue landing parachute, housed in the extended tail boom, of Su-34 Red 25 is deployed as it lands at Hmeymim air base following a bombing mission over the Syrian Arab Republic. Bottom: Su-34 Red 21 trails its landing brake parachute as it lands at Hmeymim after a bombing mission over the Syrian Arab Republic. Note the unexpended unguided bomb on the starboard engine bay station. The Aerospace Group routinely returned to base with unexpended ordnance when targets could not be confidently verified. MODRF

30 December 2015: In an area close to Mahin, Homs Province, a large hanger type structure, apparently housing a plethora of military equipment, was destroyed in a strike by at least one Su-34. Post-strike assessment showed that as well as the structure being destroyed, an infantry fighting vehicle, four trucks and five off-road vehicles, armed with large calibre machine guns, were also destroyed. The oil interdiction campaign continued with six incidences of air attacks on oil transportation vehicles in Deir-ez-Zor and Aleppo Provinces. Although the type of aircraft employed was undisclosed, this was most likely Su-24M or Su-34 (MODRF).

19 January 2016: An Su-34 attacked an ISIL position on high ground near to Kabaklia, Latakia Province. A number of direct hits with air launched munitions destroyed four off-road vehicles armed with large calibre machine guns and resulted in an estimated 20 personnel casualties. An air reconnaissance in the area of the settlement of Ahras, Aleppo Province, located a road convoy moving from an area in the region of the Turkish border toward the city Aleppo carrying reinforcements for the increasing number of extremist forces occupying the city. Su-34 strike aircraft were directed to the area, the resultant attack apparently destroying in excess of 20 off-road vehicles, resulting in undetermined armament loss and personnel casualties (MODRF).

Su-34 Red 22 of the Russian Aerospace Group adorned with markings indicating 12 mission flown over the Syrian Arab Republic. MODRF

Su-34 Red 24 (top) and an unidentified Su-34 of the Russian Aerospace group engage afterburner during take-off from Hmeymim for a night time bombing mission over the Syrian Arab Republic. The aircraft are armed with what appears to be FAB-500 M-62 general purpose 500 kg class unguided bombs. MODRF

20 January 2016: A facility near Hatla, Deir-ez-Zor Province, described by the MODRF as 'a workshop, which was used by militants for fitting vehicles with explosive devices' was destroyed by ordnance launched from at least one Su-34 (MODRF). An active artillery position was destroyed in an attack by at least one Su-34 near Meshia, Deir-ez-Zor Province. Post-strike assessment confirmed the destruction of three artillery guns (MODRF).

2 February 2016: During the course of the week leading up to 2 February 2016, Su-34's bombed in excess of ten fortified positions located on tactically important high ground near Ithriyah, Hama province while supporting Syrian army ground operations (MODRF). An ISIL fire position located on the al-Ramalyat height on the approaches to Tadmur (Palmyra), Homs province, was attacked by a Su-34. Post-strike assessment indicated that two mortar batteries and two armoured vehicles had been destroyed as a result of two direct hits by undisclosed air launched munitions (MODRF).

The major operation during this period was to relive pressure on Deir-ez-Zor, which had been besieged and was under heavy direct assault by ISIL, which was attempting to capture the town. The air operations over Deir-ez-Zor included air drops of humanitarian supplies to the inhabitants of the town by Syrian air force transport aircraft employing Russian supplied P-7 parachute-platforms. At least one Su-34 attacked a supply column consisting of ten large trucks carrying armaments and munitions from Raqqa province to Deir-ez-Zor as ISIL continued to reinforce its operations to strangle the Syrian army brigade and civilians besieged there. Post-strike assessment confirmed that all of the trucks were destroyed (MODRF).

The oil interdiction campaign continued. A small oil refinery located near Rjim al-Ammala, Raqqa Province, was destroyed by a direct hit from at least one precision guided weapon launched form a Su-34 (MODRF).

11 February 2016: A precision guided weapon launched from a Su-34 destroyed what was described as an ISIL strong point in the area of al-Ghariyah, Daraa Province. As well as the primary target, two armoured vehicles in close proximity were destroyed (MODRF).

24 February 2016: During the course of the week up to 24 February, Su-34 bombers bombed fire positions positioned on tactically important high ground near Ithriyah, Hama Province. Post-strike assessment indicated that the installations, a tank and three off-road vehicles equipped with heavy weapons, were destroyed and an estimated 50 personnel were rendered casualties. An Su-34 strike was conducted against an ISIL target at the approaches to Tadmur, near Palmyra, Homs Province. This target, a fire position on the Tlul al-Ramlayat height, was hit by two direct hits from air bombs. Post-strike assessment indicated that two crewed mortar batteries and armoured vehicles were destroyed (MODRF). A column of ten heavy trucks carrying armaments and munitions was located in Raqqa Province. Intelligence data indicated that it was bound for Deir-ez-Zor Province. This column was subsequently attacked by at least one Su-34, all ten vehicles being destroyed (MODRF).

3 March 2016: The Russian Defence Minister announced that, in accordance with an order issued by the Supreme Commander-in-Chief of the Russian Armed Forces, a significant element of the Russian armed forces grouping in Syria would be

redeployed back to bases in the Russian Federation interior commencing 15 March 2016. The first such group of aircraft, Su-34's, to leave Syria did so on 15 March, under navigational escort of a Tupolev Tu-154 transport aircraft leader. Each of the Su-34 aircraft would follow the Tu-154 formation leader until within the borders of the Russian Federation, whereafter they would proceed independently to their respective bases. If deemed necessary, the aircraft could conduct intermediate stops for refueling or for technical issues that may have arisen over the 5000+ km flights (inflight refueling being required). The Su-34's arrived at their assigned base in Voronezh region of Russia in the Western Military District later on 15 March, a series of low-level fly pasts being conducted over the base before landing to be greeted by the Commander-in-Chief of the Russian Aerospace Forces (MODRF).

Russian combat aircraft, including Su-34's, continued to fly operations over Syria through the campaigns to liberate Aleppo in 2016-2017 and Eastern Ghouta, Damascus and the drive on Deir-ez-Zor in 2017. Small-scale operations continue in 2019, against extremist organisations in Idlib Province that regularly attack outlying areas, including Aleppo, with heavy weapons, causing casualties among the civil population.

Su-34 Red 21 of the Russian Aerospace Group operating from Hmeymim air base in the Syrian Arab Republic. The aircraft is returning with unexpended ordnance indicating that at least one of its targets could not be properly identified. MODRF

GLOSSARY

ACHC	Aircraft Carrying Heavy Cruiser
Arcminute	There are 60 arcminutes in 1 degree
ASM	Air to Surface Missile
ASW	Anti-Submarine Warfare
AVMF	Soviet Naval Aviation
CEP	Circular Error Probability
CFC	Carbon Fibre Composites
CIS	Commonwealth of Independent States
cm^2	Centimetre squared
CTOL	Conventional Take-Off and Landing
DoD	Department of Defense
ECM	Electronic Counter Measures
F	Fighter
FAR	Fighter Aircraft Regiment
FBW	Fly by Wire
FCS	Flight Control System
GLONASS	Globanaya Navigozionnaya Sputnikovaya Sistema (Global Navigation Satellite System
HMTDS	Helmet Mounted Target Designation System
HP	High Pressure
HPS	Helmet Pointing System
HUD	Heads-Up-Display
IB	Istrebitel-Bombardirovshchik/fighter-bomber
Il	Ilyushin
INS/GPS	Inertial Navigation System/Global Positioning System
IRST	Infra-Red Search and Track
ISIL	Islamic State of Iraq and the Levant
KnAAPO	Komsomolsk-on-Amur production plant
LERX	Leading Edge Root Extension
l/m	Litres per minutes
LP	Low Pressure
LR	Laser Rangefinder
MANPADS	Man Portable Air Defence System
MiG	Mikoyan
MODRF	Ministry of Defence of the Russian Federation
NAPO	Novosibirsk Aviation Production Organisation
NATO	North Atlantic Treaty Organisation
NAZ	Novosibirsk Aviation Plant. V.P. Chkalova Holding

OLS	Optical Location Station
PAA	Phased Array Antenna
PAK FA	*Perspektivniy Aviacionniy Complex Frontovoi Aviacii* – Perspective Aviation Complex for Front line Aviation
POL	Petroleum Oil Lubricants
SARH	Semi-Active Radar Homing
SDF	Syrian Democratic Forces (this was a mixture of ethnic Kurds, other opposition forces and large numbers of poorly trained foreign ideologists/mercenaries – the fallacious democratic label being applied to make the organisation palatable to a western audience)
Su	Sukhoi
TsAGI	Central Aerodynamic Institute
Tu	Tupolev
TV	Television
UAC	United Aircraft Corporation
UEC	United Engine Corporation
US	United States
VKS	Russian Air Force
WSO	Weapon System Operator
°	Degree(s)
~	Approximately equal to (can also be used to mean asymptotically equal)

ABOUT THE AUTHOR

Hugh Harkins FRAS is a historian and author with an extensive research/study background in aeronautic, astronautic, astro/geophysics, nautical and the wider scientific, technical and historical fields. He is also involved in research in the field of Scottish history, which formed significant elements of dual undergraduate degrees. Hugh has published in excess of sixty books, non-fiction and fiction, writing under his given name as well as utilising several pseudonyms. He has also written for several international magazines, whilst his work has been used as reference for many other projects, ranging from the aviation industry, international news corporations and film media to encyclopaedias, museum exhibits and the computer gaming industry. Hugh is a member of the Institute of Physics and is an elected Fellow of the Royal Astronomical Society. He currently resides in his native Scotland. Other titles by the author include:

Russia's Coastal Missile Shield - Bal-E & Bastion Mobile Coastal Cruise Missile Complexes
Iskander - Mobile Tactical Aero-Ballistic/Cruise Missile Complex
Orbital/Fractional Orbit Bombardment System - The Soviet Globalnaya Raketa
Counter-Space Defence Co-Orbital Satellite Fighter
Russia's Strategic Missile Carrier/Bomber Roadmap 2018-2040 – PAK DA, Tu-160M2, Tu-95MSM & Tu-22M3M
Sukhoi T-50/PAK FA - Russia's 5th Generation 'Stealth' Fighter
Sukhoi Su-35S 'Flanker' E - Russia's 4++ Generation Super-Manoeuvrability Fighter
Sukhoi Su-34 'Fullback'
Sukhoi Su-30MKK/MK2/M2 - Russo Kitashiy Striker from Amur
Soviet Mixed Power Experimental Fighter Aircraft – Piston-Liquid Propellant Rocket Engine/Piston-Ramjet/Piston-Pulsejet & Piston-Compressor Jet Engine Designs of the 1940's
MiG-35/D 'Fulcrum' F – Towards the Fifth Generation
Air War over Syria, Tu-160, Tu-95MS & Tu-22M3 - Cruise Missile and Bombing Strikes on Syria, November 2015-February 2016
Sukhoi Su-27SM(3)/SKM
Russian/Soviet Aircraft Carrier & Carrier Aviation Design & Evolution Volume 1 - Seaplane Carriers, Project 71/72, Graf Zeppelin, Project 1123 ASW Cruiser & Project 1143-1143.4
Heavy Aircraft Carrying Cruiser
Light Battle Cruisers and the Second Battle of Heligoland Bight
British Battlecruisers of World War 1 - Operational Log, July 1914-June 1915
Eurofighter Typhoon - Storm over Europe
North American F-108 Rapier - Mach 3 Interceptor
Convair YB-60 - Fort Worth Overcast
Boeing X-36 Tailless Agility Flight Research Aircraft
X-32 - The Boeing Joint Strike Fighter
X-35 - Progenitor to the F-35 Lightning II
X-45 Uninhabited Combat Air Vehicle
Into The Cauldron - The Lancaster MK.I Daylight Raid on Augsburg
Hurricane IIB Combat Log - 151 Wing RAF, North Russia 1941
RAF Meteor Jet Fighters in World War II, an Operational Log
Typhoon IA/B Combat Log - Operation Jubilee, August 1942
Defiant MK.I Combat Log - Fighter Command, May-September 1940
Blenheim MK.IF Combat Log - Fighter Command Day Fighter Sweeps/Night Interceptions, September 1939 - June 1940
Fortress MK.I Combat Log - Bomber Command High Altitude Bombing Operations, July-September1941

www.ingramcontent.com/pod-product-compliance
Lightning Source LLC
Chambersburg PA
CBHW041521220426
43667CB00003B/57